FUNDRAISING FOR
NON-PROFIT GROUPS

FUNDRAISING FOR NON-PROFIT GROUPS

How to get money from corporations, foundations, and government

Joyce Young
Ken Wyman

(Cartoons by Charles Jaffe)

Self-Counsel Press
(a division of)
International Self-Counsel Press Ltd.
Canada   U.S.A.

Printed in Canada

*First edition: 1978
Second edition: March, 1981
Third edition: December, 1989
Reprinted: August, 1991; December, 1992
Fourth edition: October, 1995
Reprinted: June, 1996*

Canadian Cataloguing in Publication Data
Young, Joyce.
    Fundraising for non-profit groups

    (Self-counsel business series)
    First ed. published under title: Shortcuts to survival.
    ISBN 1-55180-045-4

    1. Fund raising — Canada. 2. Fund raising — United States. 3.
Corporations, Nonprofit — Canada — Finance. 4. Corporations,
Nonprofit — United States — Finance. I. Wyman, Ken. II. Title.
III. Series.
HV41.2.Y68 1995   361.7'068'1   C95-910843-2

Cover photo supplied by Digital Stock Inc.

Self-Counsel Press
(a division of)
International Self-Counsel Press Ltd.

1481 Charlotte Road
North Vancouver, B.C.
V7J 1H1

1704 N. State Street
Bellingham, Washington
98225

Dedicated to the late Max Wyman
and the newborn Max Wyman.

Each generation must make freedom, peace, and
plenty with its own hands.

CONTENTS

SAMPLES

FOREWORD

Joyce Young and Ken Wyman have been in the fundraising trenches for more than 20 years each. They have the knowledge that comes only from personal experience. They know what it's like to go eyeball to eyeball with a wealthy donor. They know what it's like to motivate a committee of volunteers who say, "I love this group. I'll do anything. Just don't ask me to raise money." They know what it's like to speak for controversial causes. Fortunately, they have decided to share their wisdom with their competition, the fundraisers of the world.

This edition of Joyce's book, with updated information from Ken, is particularly timely because fundraising has never been more challenging. The major changes in fundraising since the third edition in 1989 reflect the following changes in the world around us:

(a) Enormous increases in competition. With the end of the Cold War, the collapse of communism in Eastern Europe and the U.S.S.R., and the end of apartheid in South Africa, we have seen tens of thousands of new, non-governmental organizations or NGOs. The Third Sector is blooming in the new democracies and free market economies. Now fundraisers in the prairie provinces are competing with fundraisers in Prague and Pretoria, and fundraisers in the Maritimes are competing with fundraisers in Moscow and Minsk.

At the same time, our bother and sister fundraisers in Europe, Asia, and South America have become much more aggressive. With the improvements in telecommunications, North American charities are going to see their donors and prospects only a few digits away from good causes in Holland, Mexico, and Zimbabwe.

In 1994, there were 740,000 registered non-profits raising money in the United States, as well as tens of thousands of smaller charities, politicians, and street people asking for money. In Canada, there were about 70,000 registered charities and 60,000 other non-profit groups, about 30% to 40% more than in 1989. More competition is good for every good cause, but you must be well-organized and very clear if you want *your* good cause to get the money. This book gives you the tools to stay ahead in the global fundraising marketplace.

(b) The growing popularity of using computers. When Joyce did the first version of this book in 1978, we were using 3" × 5" cards to sort donors' names. In 1989 we were using what now seem like cheap little computers with tiny little memories but at that time seemed like Einstein in a box. Today, almost every fundraiser uses a computer to produce publications that look better, cost less, and are more fun to do than the old rubber cement and scissors system.

(c) Recognition that we are in for the long haul. The go-go eighties with the illusions of big money and quick fixes have given way to the seriousness of the 1990s and the realization that the big money comes from a lot of little gifts given faithfully over decades. Developing a broad base of small, medium, and large donors is the best way to create a permanent, powerful organization and build power to impact public policy at the same time.

Fortunately, the authors have prepared this fourth edition of *Fundraising for Non-Profit Groups* to help you, your board, and your staff survive the competition, master the new technologies, and commit to long-range strategies to achieve your fundraising goals. Worn copies of this book already grace the desks of thousands of fundraisers and they will welcome the new and updated information in this edition.

Joyce Young and Ken Wyman have proven themselves to be effective fundraisers in Canada, an immense country with a population of 29 million. A big country means higher costs to organize and a small population means more competition for volunteers and leaders. Every fundraiser working in a rural community knows this dilemma. Fundraising under these circumstances has taught Joyce and Ken to be superior organizers, motivators, and diplomats. If you want to achieve a big goal with a small group of volunteers, read this book, absorb their insights, and learn from their experiences.

The United States and Canada share the same pioneer heritage of working together to improve our communities. Worldwide, people are re-discovering and re-inventing traditions of philanthropy, generosity, and self-reliance that are centuries old. We are already willing and able to work hard. People already care enough to take action. This book gives us the tested techniques we need to work *smart* and reach the right people, to make more money, and achieve greater results with the same effort.

Joan Flanagan
Author, *The Grass Roots Fundraising Book*
and *Successful Fundraising*

ACKNOWLEDGMENTS

We want to thank our publisher and editors at Self-Counsel Press who proposed the fourth edition and supported the expansion of the book.

Our friend and colleague, Joan Flanagan, was very enthusiastic and provided invaluable advice on the manuscript. It was fun to collaborate with her.

Vicki Cowan, Daryl Sharp, and John Swaigen all took time out of their full lives to listen, read, advise, and encourage us. Their caring attention made a big difference.

Our non-profit clients over the years have made possible our learning about fundraising, management, and life. We appreciate their trust and the opportunity to walk a mile in their shoes.

J.Y.

I want to thank Joyce Young for inviting me to update her book for this fourth edition. I have long admired Joyce for her insights on fundraising, the joys and frustrations of life in the non-profit sector, and balancing work and recreation. She has inspired me (along with so many others).

Leueen MacFarlane, my wife and sometimes my work partner, has drawn me into the theological issues that are central to so many peoples' attitudes on generosity and social justice. We must always remember to think more about stewardship than fundraising. The most important issue is not extracting the money needed for this year's budget. The most important issue is helping create and sustain the belief that the world can be better, and that it is worth the time and money to be part of that invigorating, life-giving process.

Bob Bossin also inspires me with his music (Gabriola Island V0R 1X0 is the newest CD) and his dedication to teaching environmentalists how to use micro-concerts to raise money and build community. As Bob says in his song, "People like you help people like me go on."

Many non-profit groups in the United States, Canada, and around the world deserve my thanks for openly sharing their troubles with me so we could work together to develop solutions. Each of us learn from those who went before.

Self-Counsel Press, our publisher, and Natasha Young, our editor, deserve thanks for keeping this book current and widely in circulation, and for their patience in waiting for the manuscript while my office recovered after our computers were stolen. (If you haven't backed up your computer files lately, go do it right now!)

I want to thank *you* for reading this book, and, I hope, putting some of our ideas into action. Joyce and I aren't doing this for the money. Our chief gratification is hearing from groups that use our ideas to make the world better. Drop us a note.

K.W.

INTRODUCTION

a. THE MISSION

This book is about financing social change. It is about finding the dollars to help you make this world a better place — however you define that.

The fourth edition of *Fundraising* is a timely renewal, because the 1990s has been a decade of rapid social change. The Kent State protesters of the sixties are now the politicians and corporate vice presidents of the 1990s, and I don't believe their values have changed. As Environics pollster Michael Adams put it, "I predict that the elite critique of the sixties will be mainstream thinking in the 1990s, tempered by the realities of our collective experiences over the past two decades." Those social forces make the 1990s a decade of active social change. Even if you disagree, you will acknowledge that the "baby boomers" represent enormous financial and leadership potential for social change through public interest groups.

Fundraising is about building understanding, discovering common ground, and ensuring a "win-win" outcome. It's about finding the fit between volunteers and organizations, between needs and donors. Fundraising is also about taking responsibility for something out there that's not right, and acting on it. It's about empowering others, be they volunteer fundraisers, clients, or advocates.

People want to give, they want to belong to something bigger than themselves, and they want to spend their money on things with purpose and meaning. The challenge of fundraising is to connect person with person first. Then ask, and the money will come. But you do have to ask.

It is essential that fundraisers and board members put pride and power into fundraising. In the past, there has been a tendency to view it as the dirty work of non-profit organizations, somewhat sleazy and manipulative, or to view it as begging. Any seasoned fundraiser will tell you that guilt only works once, and begging doesn't work at all! We need to put pride and power into fundraising because that's where the money comes from, and without money, an organization can't achieve its mission.

Fundraising demands discipline from an organization, and that is needed in public interest groups. Undisciplined passion may be great at demonstrations, but it doesn't build an organization with the staying power to achieve social change. The need to raise money is often the driving force for strategic planning, financial planning, and program design and evaluation.

We have a favorite saying about fundraising: The biggest problem with fundraising is that people don't do it. They worry about it. They talk about it. They read books and hold committee meetings about it. But they don't DO IT. Our goal with this book is to help you, encourage you, and, most of all, make you DO IT! Fundraising works. It will work for you if you only DO IT!

b. WHO THIS BOOK IS FOR

Fundraising is for people who want to know how to go about raising between $100,000 and $5 million annually for a charitable, non-profit group. This is the kind of price range we are familiar with. If you want to raise more money than you do now, raise money from different sources, or try a new fundraising technique, this book gets you started.

If you sit on the board of directors of a non-profit group, the information in this book helps you better understand your role and assess the fundraising efforts and strategies of your group. This new edition of *Fundraising* also discusses management because fundraising and management are inseparable. As fundraising consultants, we've found that fundraising difficulty was often a symptom of management problems. This book describes ways to integrate fundraising and management functions.

For groups that are just starting or want to hire fundraising staff, this book paints a detailed picture of the task ahead. Fundraising strategies for public interest groups that are perceived to be controversial, innovative, or non-traditional are emphasized throughout.

c. WHAT THIS BOOK CAN (AND CAN'T) DO FOR YOU

Fundraising is easy to understand, simple, and direct. It demystifies fundraising and gets you going. This book is lean and mean, just like your organization.

The demand for the charitable dollar far exceeds the supply of money and the number of non-profit groups continues to grow. There are about 70,000 registered charities and 60,000 other non-profit groups in Canada, and about 740,000 in the United States. You are *competing* for the charitable dollar and the competition is keen. Well-organized, well-established, and well-known large charities probably already have their chunk of any corporation's or foundation's donations budget secured, so your group is competing for the 5% to 30% of the budget that is left over. That's not very encouraging, but it's best to know what you are up against. With the help of this book, you will have a head start in the race for dollars.

This book takes you through the practical and strategic steps of fundraising from preparing a proposal to recruiting a fundraising committee. It tells you what kind of information the potential sponsor wants to see and how to present it. Three essential fundraising tools — the objectives sheet, the

3

annual report, and the funding proposal — are covered in detail with examples.

After you have put together your fundraising tools, who should you ask for money? To answer that, you need to develop a funding strategy. Figuring out a logical and solid funding strategy is the most challenging, the most difficult, and the most important part of fundraising. Chapter 5 provides a step-by-step explanation with examples of the process.

We deal with raising money from individuals, corporations, foundations, and government sources. Corporate fundraising is covered in depth, because that's where many groups lack knowledge and experience. In chapter 6, the subtleties and the tricks of getting in the door to see a funder are discussed. On the other hand, many controversial groups have to rely heavily on individuals for support. Therefore, direct mail campaigns and telephone fundraising are explained, and an example of a direct mail package is included.

How to keep the money coming is an important part of any fundraising program, so examples of reporting and record-keeping systems are provided. If you have a deficit, *Fundraising* tells you how to cope with that problem and get out of it.

As volunteers are the lifeblood of many groups, a chapter is devoted to developing a solid volunteer network.

This book won't make you rich in five easy steps; if you expect to get rich, you're in the wrong business. But it will tell you all the things we wish we had known when we began fundraising, and what we have learned in 20 very busy years of fundraising and fundraising consulting. This book tells you what you need to know about fundraising so that your group can thrive and accomplish change.

1

THE FUNDRAISER

Good fundraisers are hard to find and harder to keep. Often they are given too many conflicting responsibilities. A relationship between the fundraiser and group that works well is outlined in this chapter.

a. THE FUNDRAISER'S ROLE

The fundraiser should have an integral part in management and decision making and should not be just a "money magnet" stuck in a corner and told to bring in the bucks. Advice on the "fund-ability" of a proposed project should carry substantial weight in decision making. An experienced fundraiser should not be told to raise money for something he or she considers "unfundable."

Management theory clearly supports the fundraiser's involvement in decision making. Your fundraiser has to sell to the prospective donor your organization's vision, mandate, program, and budget. That's not possible if he or she isn't included in thinking these things through. We can take a lesson from the private sector here. "Inadequate product knowledge" is cited as one of the most frequent reasons for failure in sales. To sell the organization, your fundraiser has to believe in it. He or she has to be a part of the team, has to be brought in on the mission, the direction, the program design. Does business exclude its marketing people from the design of new products? Hardly! Important management decisions have fundraising implications, and vice versa. Don't make them in isolation!

It is important that your fundraiser be determined to raise the money, but not at any cost. If the fundraiser has to compromise on your group's principles or misrepresent your group to funders in order to get money, it's money you don't want. There are degrees of compromise, of course, but you can't let funding interfere with your mandate. Therefore, you want a fundraiser whose first commitment is to your cause. Raising money is the means that makes possible the end; it is not an end in itself.

How much money a full-time fundraiser can be expected to raise depends on many factors, including the following:

(a) Whether your group is controversial

(b) Whether you have a track record in fundraising

(c) Whether you have any annual lump-sum funding

(d) What funding sources and fundraising techniques you will use

Think of your fundraiser as a salesperson. How much your fundraiser can sell depends not only on his or her skills, but also on the market and the product. The market is your potential donors, the product is your organization or program. Too many fundraisers take the blame for a poor product.

Raising $2 million for a university may take the same amount of work as raising $100,000 for an anti-nuclear lobby or a breast cancer support group. To get a realistic picture of the amount of money your fundraiser can be expected to raise, contact another group similar to yours and find out what its experience has been. There are simply too many variables to give a general guideline.

Your fundraiser must keep up with new developments in your issue area and current issues in the business and philanthropic communities. If the corporate sector provides a substantial part of your income, the *Financial Post* or

Wall Street Journal and the business section of a major daily newspaper are required reading.

The fundraiser's administrative duties should be limited to financial transactions. He or she must plan your income and supervise cash flow and expenditures. In a small organization, all checks should require the fundraiser's signature and one other signature. That way he or she can make sure you aren't overdrawn at the end of the month. If your group has an annual budget of more than $100,000, an office manager or executive director will need to be involved in financial administration. The fundraiser must be involved in planning cash flow. Maintaining cash flow is one of the best incentives to get the fundraiser working hard.

b. HIRING A FUNDRAISER

When you look for a fundraiser, you are looking for a personality — a personality that can cope with pressure, demands, some ingratitude, and many disappointments. You need a self-motivated person who can work closely with your group.

Some universities and colleges now offer courses in fundraising which are very useful, but the most meaningful credential is previous experience. Make sure that the candidate's experience is relevant to your needs and your sources of income. A person who can organize successful benefit concerts may not do well at government fundraising.

Fundraisers should be effective, agile communicators. In fundraising meetings, they need to impress and influence a wide range of people. The fundraiser must be able to conduct a discussion smoothly and lead it to a positive conclusion — money! But beware of people who only talk a good line — too often they can't produce results. You want an honest and hard worker in this position particularly.

Good, straightforward writing skills are essential. Fundraisers write letters and proposals all the time. The writing must be interesting, clear, and concise, because boring proposals won't get read. Ask to see samples of the candidate's writing or make a writing assignment part of your hiring process.

Your fundraiser must look presentable in a business setting and should be as comfortable in a designer suit as in blue jeans.

When you are interviewing people for the fundraising job, get a successful fundraiser from another group to sit in. The outside fundraiser can ask the tough questions and objectively assess candidates. If you are desperate to find a fundraiser, this outside perspective could spare you the cost of a poor decision made in haste.

The fundraiser's most important duty is to mobilize volunteers who will do the actual fundraising work. Fundraisers who do the work themselves are quickly overwhelmed and burned out. Even when they are successful, they are not strengthening the diversity of people and skills that are essential to a non-profit's stability. No organization can survive if it depends on just one person's skills, knowledge, or contacts. One day the fundraiser will leave. The organization should be more self-reliant and independent long before that day comes.

c. FIRING A FUNDRAISER

All staff in non-profit groups should have probation periods. You can't afford dreamers and shirkers, you need people who can produce. There should be no such thing as tenure in non-profit groups.

When interviewing fundraising applicants, describe the probation period clearly. For the fundraising position, a period of six to twelve months is reasonable. It takes up to six months to get decisions on funding requests. It's only fair to give fundraisers that much time to prove themselves.

8

If your group is new, or new to fundraising, a six-month probation period for a fundraiser is too short. It will take time for your group to establish a reputation in the funding community. A fundraiser for a new group should be given at least a year and should be judged initially by the amount of work he or she is putting out, not results.

However, if you aren't getting the dollar results within six to twelve months, you must act. Few concerns raise the collective blood pressure of a board of directors as high as the issue of firing someone. Firing, dismissal, termination — call it what you will — is fraught with a level of emotional upheaval comparable only to the stir that a lawsuit or near-bankruptcy evokes.

Because it's such a difficult thing to handle well, firing is usually mismanaged in one of two ways:

(a) The board puts its head in the sand, holds its breath, and prays that the whole nasty business will go away.

(b) The board gathers the courage to fire the person and handles the firing badly.

Let's look at each scenario in turn.

1. The head in the sand

If the problem is serious enough to warrant high-level attention in the first place, odds are that it will escalate if left unattended. When you start getting complaints from staff or board members who do not normally call you directly, you know the problem has grown. If staff start to resign, you likely have a situation that needs fast, decisive action.

2. How not to fire someone

How the firing is handled has a tremendous impact on many facets of the organization. Whether the employee you fire bad-mouths the organization or brings a legal suit is not all there is to it. It affects morale and is the sort of thing board members resign over. It affects your organization's reputation with clients, with funders, and with regulatory agencies. It will also affect your ability to attract good candidates to fill the job.

Here are some examples of handling termination badly:

(a) The whole board is involved in the decision to fire the employee. Can you imagine what that does for the employee's reputation? How would you like to be fired by 10 or 20 people?

(b) The employee first learns about it from a subordinate, a well-intentioned board member who leaks the information, or the morning paper.

(c) From the employee's perspective, it happens out of the blue: no feedback, no warning, no opportunity to improve performance.

(d) The employee is not given the option of resigning and leaving with confidentiality and dignity.

3. Pointers for terminating employment

Following are some suggestions on how to tackle this unpleasant task so that everyone emerges with dignity:

(a) Prevention: boards are often guilty of doing too little too late. Take action and give attention to the small problems as they arise, before they escalate.

(b) See that the procedure for dealing with termination is spelled out, either in your contract with your employee or your personnel policy.

(c) Keep the number of people who know about the situation and who are involved in making the firing decision as small as possible.

(d) For the few people who are involved in the decision, allow the time that is needed to work through each person's thoughts and feelings on the matter. Give your group all the information it needs to make an informed decision. Fear and ignorance in this area is the main reason for a head-in-the-sand response. It will go more smoothly if you can come to consensus and each person truly believes it is the only solution, or the best solution.

(e) Get legal advice from a lawyer who knows employment law. Termination is a complex matter and the legalities depend on the specifics of each case. Find out where you stand.

Few people will pat you on the back for doing a good job of firing somebody, but you aren't an ogre with an axe. You are a leader who isn't afraid to put the well-being of your organization ahead of your own popularity. You won't win an award for this one, but you will deserve one if you handle it well.

2

ORGANIZING FOR EFFECTIVE FUNDRAISING

a. ARE VOLUNTEER ORGANIZATIONS DIFFERENT?

Some people think the voluntary sector is a nice, sheltered place to work. After all, we are going to make a better world and, besides, the non-profit sector is not "the real world." Right?

Wrong! Non-profits are not nice, sheltered places to work. They are the toughest organizations to participate in. There is more uncertainty, complexity, difference, and conflict — and far fewer resources to deal with it, so be proud and stand tall for doing this kind of work. The non-profit sector does not have a monopoly on making the world a better place, and the attitude that it does alienates a lot of potential partners in government, in foundations, and in industry.

There *are* differences between volunteer organizations and profit-based companies, however, and these differences have nothing to do with one sector being "better" or "easier" than the other. The following examples illustrate this point.

After one turbulent board meeting, a client said to Joyce, "If any of my staff ever pulled a stunt like that I'd fire them. They would be out of here! But you can't fire a volunteer. You can't tell them what to do either. It has to be *consensus!*" He was a vice president of Xerox who was 18 months into his first experience on the board of a volunteer organization.

Joyce's neighbor, who makes her living as a management consultant and who was recruited to the board of a community organization, called in quite a stir. "Joyce, I can't believe it," she said. "The meeting starts 15 minutes late and for the next half hour people continue to arrive. The chairperson interrupts the meeting to welcome them, asks how their kids are doing, and then brings them up to speed on what we were discussing. I don't know how a place can function with a board like that!"

Many of you will recognize the "culture shock" of these new initiates. You may remember learning the ropes in your organization: it wasn't what you'd expected. Ask anybody who has been a board, committee, or staff member, and they will agree that volunteer organizations are different from profit-making companies.

Does it matter? Yes, because if you can grasp why and how volunteer organizations are fundamentally different, important possibilities emerge. The possibility of doing more with less, of being more effective with the same level of resources. The possibility of structuring the organization in ways that will provide timely decisions and better coordination. The possibility of ensuring longer-term, productive volunteers. The possibility of predicting conflict and crisis so you can better manage it. The possibility of moving beyond a hand-to-mouth financial existence.

By looking at four important aspects of non-profit groups, you will begin to understand *why* they are different.

1. Volunteer labor

A new manufacturing organization will start out by *borrowing money* which it uses to hire the staff and buy the raw materials and the technology it needs to manufacture a product. It then sells the product to the consumer. The money from sales is fed back into the organization to maintain production and to pay for the cost of the borrowed money. In time, the start-up debt is repaid. In a very simple and general way, that's how a private company gets started.

13

Now, look at the volunteer group. The founders begin the organization by *donating labor* which is used to provide a product or service to a consumer, often for free. No money may change hands in these early stages, or if it does, it is usually money which is "given" by the same people who give the labor.

Those are very different scenarios. The fact that the volunteer organization began with the free labor of its founders might explain a few things. Consider this example. The hypothetical ZIP Organization began with John, Mary, Elsie, and a few others meeting in each other's living rooms on Monday nights. Then more people got interested, ZIP grew, and the members started meeting down in the church basement. Well, it was such a helpful thing and word spread and pretty soon there were Monday night meetings in church basements all over the city.

If you project this flourishing organization seven years into the future, you might witness the following. It is the meeting of the provincial board of ZIP, which now has 12 chapters. The executive director is presenting her proposed budget for the next fiscal year. It includes a 7% salary increase, the addition of health and dental benefits, the purchase of liability insurance, and the purchase of a computer and a photocopy machine. Then there's the $1,000 for rental of a hotel conference room to hold the annual general meeting.

John, Mary, and Elsie are exchanging glances across the 20-person oak boardroom table on the 34th floor of a downtown office building. They aren't too enthusiastic about this budget and they are wondering how it came to this. It's still Monday night, but this is no church basement!

When an organization changes from being led and run by volunteers to having a financial life of its own, the founders are displaced. They don't own the organization anymore. Often, they don't even understand or recognize it anymore.

The start-up debt, which is still owed to founders like John, Mary, and Elsie, is an emotional debt. It can only be repaid by giving recognition and respect to the founders and to their vision and values for the organization. The importance of this goes beyond keeping your founders happy and preventing them from reacting and trying to maintain control. The vision and values that gave a few people the energy to give birth to a new organization will help to sustain that organization. The vision will evolve, but the original vision should serve as an anchor, keeping the organization directed and purposeful.

The fact that most volunteer organizations begin with volunteer labor rather than venture capital and are financed indirectly by a third party, the funders, may be the beginning of the following chronic problems:

(a) The start-up debt is hidden and not repaid. The start-up debt is what is owed to the founding members who got it all rolling in the first place.

(b) Staff are underpaid — the only variable is how badly underpaid they are. The staff or board may even believe it is virtuous to be underpaid. The board members are often those who used to do the staff's work without pay, so they view staff work as replacing their free labor. The problem of uncompetitive salaries manifests itself in problems ranging from incompetence to high turnover.

(c) Volunteer organizations are undercapitalized. They do not have the equipment they need to do the job and thus much valuable volunteer time is wasted running errands. Productivity is low, which makes it harder to raise funds, which means no equipment can be bought, and the vicious cycle continues.

2. Funding

A second point of comparison is the difference in the sources of money for the two types of organizations. In profit-making companies, the consumer has the choice whether to purchase a product in the first place, and whether to purchase your brand or a competitor's. The first choice depends on the need for the product or service, and the second choice depends on aspects of quality, availability, and price. Consumers' dollars are the major source of funds for the company and the consumers' buying behavior gives the company feedback about how well it's doing, imposing a standard on the quality of the product or service. If a product does not meet the consumers' standards, the company knows immediately by a drop in sales. If it does not adjust to the needs of its customers, it will go out of business.

If you look at these same variables in volunteer organizations, you will see that they operate very differently. First, there is often the absence of a direct and visible consumer. In the case of an advocacy organization, if we say that their "product" is information, it would be clear that the users of that information are politicians, government organizations, and private corporations. However, the people who benefit from their efforts are an entirely different group.

Even when there is something approaching a consumer, the service is often free. Rarely does another group offer the same service to the same consumer group, so there is no competition for consumers. Finally, the money for all of this is provided by a third party funder, such as a foundation or government agency.

What does all this add up to? It means that the funders' and the volunteer organizations' criteria become the measure of "need" and "quality of service" and "efficiency" — not the consumers' criteria. In some cases, what the consumers want and what the funders will fund are in absolute conflict. The volunteer organization is in the middle of that conflict. In addition, the organization and the funders don't get the kind of direct feedback from the consumers that a drop in revenue provides to a profit-based company. These facts can become the source of many problems and the only solution we know is to try to get funders and clients together. This is happening with some U.S. foundations that are getting trustees out into the field and getting clients into their boardrooms.

3. Values

Volunteer organizations are *value driven*. The logic of what your organization does is often based on an unarticulated, emotional, personal, nebulous thing called values. Members of the group are driven by their commitment to those values. The power of shared values to motivate and coordinate people is so great that many corporations are trying to emulate it.

Ultimately, however, money-making companies are profit-driven. They may be ethical corporations with high moral standards, but their primary goal is still to make money. Therefore, if a question of values arises, the company will not necessarily be torn apart by this conflict. A value-driven, volunteer organization, on the other hand, could very well be destroyed by such a conflict. Though they may share a general goal, all members of an organization do not have exactly the same values, and when the differences between their values become greater than the similarities, the organization is in trouble.

In order for the power of values to work for your group, the board and the staff need to be able to talk about values and work them through. You need to recognize value conflicts when they arise, and confront them fast. This calls for a lot of interpersonal strength and maturity.

4. Volunteer leadership

Non-profits are volunteer-led organizations. While in the past decade staff have become more sophisticated and professional, boards continue to be made up of people from many levels of society. This difference leads to increased board-staff conflict and conflict within the board itself. Conflict in an organization can be healthy, provided you learn to express it and deal with it. Conflict can also take over your whole agenda, and then you need outside help.

b. INCORPORATION AND CHARITABLE REGISTRATION

This section is not a definitive work on the topic; it will not tell you whether you should incorporate or how to do it. You should seek a lawyer's advice on that. This section simply gives a basic overview and points out the fundraising implications of incorporation and charitable registration.

Incorporation means constituting your group as a legal entity separate and distinct from your membership or board of directors. It establishes your group as a more permanent structure and limits the personal liability of the staff and the board.

In Canada and the U.S., you can incorporate at the state or provincial level. Provincial or state incorporation is more flexible, has fewer regulations and reporting requirements, and can be accomplished more quickly and inexpensively. You will probably need a lawyer's help, but you may be able to find a lawyer who is sympathetic to your cause and will do the job as a public service. (For more information on Canadian organizations, see *Forming and Managing a Non-Profit Organization*, another title in the Self-Counsel Series.)

Corporations and foundations prefer to fund incorporated groups; many require incorporation. Non-profit corporations are perceived to be more permanent, accountable, and credible. Funders feel that a donation to an incorporated group is safer and that there will be a long-term benefit from their charitable investment.

If you are in Canada and the activities of your group are of a "charitable" nature (i.e., religious, educational, scientific, artistic, or social), you can apply to Revenue Canada for tax exemption registration. (This is called charitable registration throughout the book.) If your application is accepted, you will be issued a charitable registration number. This number entitles you to issue receipts for tax credits for donations. It also exempts you from paying federal and provincial sales tax on printed, educational materials.

In the United States, not-for-profit corporations can apply for federal tax exemption under section 501(c)(3) of the Internal Revenue Code. If you expect to be around for a few years and your annual budget will exceed $25,000, you will probably want to incorporate.

Neither in Canada nor the United States do you have to incorporate to obtain charitable registration status, but the documentation requirements for a non-profit corporation are virtually the same as for an unincorporated association.

Charities and fundraising activities are closely regulated in the United States. The first step is to incorporate in the state in which you operate. Then contact the Internal Revenue Service and ask about filing for federal tax exemption under section 501(c)(3) of the Internal Revenue Code. The government has four free publications dealing with tax exempt status which you can order through your local IRS tax forms office. Ask for Package 1023, Publication 557, and Form 8718. For those who need to know tax technicalities, you can order the IRS agents' own manual on exempt organizations. Contact the government printing office in Washington D.C. and ask for IRS Manual Section 7751.The application will require information on your objects, by-laws, board of directors, and funding base. You probably need the help of a lawyer.

You need to examine the legislation affecting your group at the state level. Many states now have legislation affecting matters such as:

(a) The composition of your funding base

(b) The requirements for reporting contributions received

(c) The percentage of your total budget required for fundraising costs

(d) The licensing of fundraisers or of fundraising consultants

CHARITABLE REGISTRATION STATUS IS AN ABSO-
LUTE PREREQUISITE FOR RAISING MONEY FROM COR-
PORATIONS AND FOUNDATIONS.

Charitable registration is not required by most government funding sources. In fact, if you get a grant from a
government source, do not issue them a receipt for a tax
credit for the donation — it will only confuse them.

Annual membership fees are not tax deductible in Canada.
You can issue receipts for donations over and above the membership fee. When doing membership or direct mail campaigns,
you should distinguish between membership fees and donations. Include a box for the donor to indicate if he or she wants
a tax credit receipt issued. The canceled check is a sufficient
receipt in the United States, for donations under $250 in a single
gift. The IRS allows membership fees to be fully or partly tax
deductible, depending on the benefits a member receives. The
tax laws change regularly, however, so check with your local
tax office about the best way to proceed.

For a more detailed discussion of incorporation and
charitable registration, consult one of the reference works
listed in the Appendix.

c. BOARD OF DIRECTORS

A board of directors is a legal necessity if you want to
incorporate. You are required to have a minimum number of
directors but you can set the maximum. Your bylaws state
how many directors your organization can have; the bylaws
can be amended, if desired, at your annual general meeting.

If you want to get a lot of help from your board, you
should give a lot of thought to whom you choose and how
you recruit them. Remember that the board member is a
volunteer. Chapter 12, which discusses working with volunteers, also applies to working with board members.

1. Who should be on the board?

The board is an important part of your business identity. Prominent, respected people in your field of endeavor should be on the board. If your group is controversial, these people are doubly important because they lend credibility to your existence and activities.

Your board may be a "figurehead" board or a "working" board, or a combination of both. Figurehead board members satisfy legal necessity and business credibility, but do not have much involvement in the day-to-day running of the group. Working board members get their hands dirty and work closely with the staff. Figurehead board members lend you their good names, and working board members give you their time.

Many groups find it useful to create a separate group called something like "The Friends of Martian Mice." This can be populated by people prepared to devote their energy to fundraising. They don't take the power away from the working board, or, as it is sometimes called, the managing board. This also means the non-profit doesn't have to try the often impossible task of transforming existing board members (who may have many wonderful skills) into fundraisers. Nor do they have to fear that fundraising leaders, who may not understand the issues as well, will wreak havoc on the board. Larger organizations often institutionalize the "Friends of" by turning it into a legal foundation. Hospitals and universities do this a lot.

It is a good idea to have a lawyer and an accountant on your board. They may do your legal work and your books at cost or for free, but their importance goes beyond that. Every business has a lawyer and an accountant because these people are necessary. They help to round out your business identity, and they can warn you of the legal or financial implications of projects you are planning.

Recruit at least two board members who are outside "the cause" of your organization. Outsiders will give time to your organization for many different reasons. A volunteer accountant once said, "I wanted to do something with more meaning and purpose than helping the rich get richer." At the board meeting of a bereaved parents' group, a newly recruited outsider said simply, "There, but for the grace of God, go I...." You may not expect it, but you *can* recruit outsiders and they are invaluable. Every cause has its blind spots, which only outsiders can see. Blind spots are values, beliefs, attitudes, and assumptions that don't work in the outside world. By recognizing and challenging the blind spots, the outsiders can help your group to see them and correct them. Funders don't like blind spots.

You need two strong board members who will champion fundraising, make it fun and exciting and sexy, and give it prestige and resources. Fundraising must be a strategic, mainstream function at the board and staff level. Give the fundraising function a power base within the board of directors. I've seen too many boards give low or no priority to fundraising, and then cry help when they "suddenly discover" the group is in the red. Find the board leadership that fundraising needs and deserves. Draw on sales and marketing people from the private sector.

Last, but by no means least, you should have a few business people on your board. The lack of business people on boards of lobby groups and arts groups is a common shortcoming. Business people can help you with fundraising, but if you want them to help raise funds, you should indicate this when you invite them to be on your board. Find out what kind of commitment they are willing to make. If they are willing to help with fundraising, they can do the following:

(a) Directly solicit prospective donors on your behalf.

(b) Go with you to fundraising meetings with important potential funders. The fact that the board members are willing to invest that kind of time indicates to the potential sponsor that they are very committed to your group. It also puts more peer pressure on the potential donor.

(c) Write to those people on your behalf, indicating their involvement with your group and requesting that they take the time to meet with you. (This doesn't guarantee any money, but it usually means that you will get a meeting and a chance to make a pitch for money.)

(d) Suggest senior people in the business community who they think would be sympathetic or interested in your cause.

You should select all board members because of their commitment to your cause. You don't want a token lawyer; you want a lawyer who is interested in your field of endeavor. You don't want a businessperson who is only there to "be seen" as a good corporate citizen; you want someone who cares about your cause and will invest time and energy to see it succeed. It's a real balancing act to assemble a board that has diversity and cohesion.

Have a few business people on your board.

23

Board members cannot be paid for serving on your board but, generally, paid staff members can be members of the board. Don't put too many staffers on the board, however; a staff-dominated board makes funders nervous. From their point of view, there's not enough control or accountability in staff-dominated boards.

2. Recruiting board members

Once you find a candidate for the board, the chairperson should try to find the board job that best fits the potential member. Then the chair should approach the candidate by spending some time with him or her, explaining the history and goals of the organization. The chair should ask if the candidate is willing to make a commitment to attend all board meetings, to take on his or her share of the legal responsibility, and to spend time working on special projects or committees of the board, like the fundraising committee.

If the candidate responds positively, he or she should be introduced to staff and key volunteers, tour the office, be brought up to date on recent plans and activities, and be introduced to the other board members. This way, the newcomer will be well oriented in the organization.

It is better to have a steady flow of retirements from the board and new people coming in than to have to replace the whole board at once. Some groups set a "term" for board members and have to replace them all when the term is up. This is most common where the board members are elected by the general membership. It's best to have board members and staff work on recruiting new board members before others retire. This provides continuity. You might even try to get the retiring members to find their own replacements, if they are good. This assumes that the board is not democratically elected but largely self-appointed, which is often the case.

When people decide to leave the board, it is important to let them retire gracefully. If people are made to feel guilty when they want to leave, that leaves a sour taste from their volunteer experience, and they will be more reluctant to volunteer for something else. You can't expect the same people to do all the work, all the time, forever. It is usually true that 20% of the people do 80% of the work, but you have to keep the membership of that 20% dynamic by allowing those who feel they have done their part to step down and by bringing in new energy.

3. Responsibilities of the board

The responsibilities of the board can be divided into two main categories: policy and management.

(a) Policy

The board should develop both short range and long range goals to help your group fulfill its mission and it should decide priorities for spending funds. It should regularly evaluate programs, staff and volunteer performance, and its own performance. It should also represent and promote the organization within the community.

The extent to which the board of directors sets or controls policy and positions on issues will vary from group to group. Whether or not they exercise it, the directors do have the ultimate decision-making power and responsibility for the group and its actions. If they are experienced and committed directors, their advice on the management and direction of the group can be very valuable; they have both experience and perspective which the staff often lacks.

(b) Management

Planning the budget, planning and supervising the fundraising (if not actually doing a lot of it), ensuring that expenditures are kept within the budget and that projects are carried out on schedule, and seeing that financial records are kept are all functions of the board. It may delegate some of this work to staff, but the board is ultimately accountable for legal obligations.

The board will hire and fire senior staff and may also recruit important volunteers. It is the board's job to resolve any internal conflicts between board members or between board and staff members. If there is a serious dispute and the people can't work it out, a member of the board should deal with it quickly. The longer you wait, the harder it gets.

Many groups list the board of directors on their letterhead. When you are starting out, the only credibility you may be able to demonstrate is your board of directors.

List more than the names of your board members. The more potential donors know about your board, the more credible your organization becomes.

A board member named "Jane Doe" might be anybody. Add any degrees so potential donors can be reassured that you have a lawyer and an accountant on the team. Note other "respectable" titles, such as doctors, clergy, other health professionals, and so on. "The Rev. Dr. Jane Doe, Ph.D., M.Div., B.S.W." is much more impressive.

Show where the people work to further identify them. It can provide the added credibility by association with another organization. "The Rev. Dr. Jane Doe, Ph.D., M.Div., B.S.W., President, Utopia University" adds credibility.

Some people worry that this discriminates against valuable people who have fewer of these socially acceptable credentials. A mini-biography of those people may solve this problem. For example a group like Artists for Fair Wages might list "John Row, full-time artist for ten years."

4. Board development

Although the board has all of these duties, some board members aren't very good at carrying out these functions. This is where the chairperson and the executive director should work very closely.

If board members aren't coming to meetings or aren't working, the chair of the board should try to encourage them to contribute more. If that doesn't work, find a tactful way to get them to resign and replace them with people who are willing to work.

Sometimes board members lack skills in matters like running a meeting, making decisions, setting policy, or dealing with finances. They may have expertise in understanding and relating to the community, but lack these management skills. The executive director and the chairperson can get together and work out a plan for board development, which is a nice way of saying training. The training needs to be approached in a way that won't offend the respected board members, so it helps to have the chairperson involved with it.

Board development might consist of a simple presentation on how to make decisions in a group, how to chair a meeting, how to do a budget, or different methods of fundraising. Staff can do informal board training by making presentations on topics they have studied in courses. However you go about it, board training is a necessary investment. The Canadian Centre for Philanthropy or the Foundation Center can help you to find competent trainers. So can the United Way. In many communities there are now college courses on fundraising or volunteer management.

The book *Working With Volunteer Boards* is a great help on this topic. It is available from Volunteer Ontario (see the address in the Appendix).

5. Committees

One way to reduce the board's workload is by creating working committees, such as a fundraising committee or a management committee, made up of a few working members of your board. Committee membership, however, does not have to be limited to board members. Board members heading up a committee can recruit new members from outside the board; this is a good way of bringing in new people. For example, a fundraising committee could be composed of one or two board members and a number of prominent members of the business community recruited by your board members. Later, committee members might be invited to join the board when there is a vacancy.

A fundraising committee can be of great help to you, but before you rush off to arrange it, ask yourself whether a committee structure is going to be any more effective than volunteers working individually for the organization. For a committee to be effective, you need business people with clout, and people with clout are busy. It's more important that these people go out and raise money for you than spend time in committee meetings. Arranging committee meetings and reporting on them also takes your time, and your time is valuable. Don't assume the structure; design the structure to suit your own needs and the needs of your volunteers.

d. MANAGING GROWTH

The rapid growth and expansion of organizations is more of a problem in the voluntary sector than you might think. It seems we are so accustomed to a "struggle and survive" mentality that when growth knocks on the door, we are immediately seduced. Growth can derail an organization just as quickly as bankruptcy, so you should know what it looks like and how to manage it.

First, get a perspective on the growth of your organization. Comparing your group to another in the same field or same community won't help. Where you are now, compared to a year ago — or a year hence, is what matters. Indicators of growth in your organization include increases in —

  (a) your annual operating budget,

  (b) the number of chapters, branches, or divisions,

  (c) the number of volunteers and paid staff,

(d) the number of new programs or services,

(e) your fundraising projections, or

(f) your sphere of influence.

These are just a few general "growth and change" parameters for your organization that will help you identify and quantify growth in an objective and rational way.

Organizations can experience two kinds of growth: organic and artificial. Organic growth is an orderly and incremental development that arises naturally from within the organization. It will cause some growing pains but it's manageable. Artificial growth is created by a major change *outside* the organization. New legislation, new technology, new major funding sources, or a suddenly elevated social or political profile are only a few of the external changes that can spark artificial growth.

Artificial growth is explosive, fast-changing, and, often, out of control. It is compelling and seductive; it begs you to accommodate it. It requires astute management to keep it harnessed and directed. If you are looking at doubling your annual budget in one year, hiring five or more paid staff for the first time, adding three new target groups or services, or merging with another organization, you are dealing with artificial growth.

Recently, Joyce consulted with several groups who were facing at least three of these items in their next fiscal year. Only one of them managed to say "No" to artificial growth. This group could see that they would burn out their volunteer base, program quality would suffer, and the reputation they had worked so hard to build would be at risk. So instead they chose to work at expanding their volunteer base first. They plan to be able to properly accommodate half of the originally projected growth a year from now.

Artificial growth is not bad and you should not decline it, but you must recognize it as a major change and understand it is not necessarily desirable. Carefully assess both the opportunities and the risks it poses for your organization. Then make a deliberate decision about whether to take it on and how you will manage it.

e. NETWORKING

Networking has become an essential activity for job seekers, fundraisers, managers — everybody. It is a powerful tool for getting access to important people or information and for building coalitions. It is a way of doing more with less. Unfortunately, some networkers have forgotten, or never knew, the rules of the game.

A network is an informal system of one-to-one, face-to-face relationships. Information and access are the business of the network. There is a set of shared values and goals, a sense of kindred spirit and colleagueship that holds a network together. Without that, you don't have a real network.

There are three roles that members of the network can fulfill: "Asker," "Giver," or "Link," and there are rules for each role.

If you are the Asker, your first task is to be specific and realistic about what you want from the Giver. You should do everything possible to make it *easy* for the Giver to help you, and knowing precisely what you want is the first step. Another way to make it easy for the Giver is to ask for time on the phone, rather than a meeting. Respect the Giver's time, and intrude as little as possible. Finally, if the Giver helps you, a brief note explaining what happened is a must. That's how you say "thank you."

There are rules for Givers, too. Sometimes Givers just give out a lot of advice without taking the time to listen carefully to the Asker and determine the Asker's needs. Too often, Givers promise something and then don't deliver. It's better to simply say "no" in the first place.

Finally, there are the Links, the people who connect the Askers to the Givers. The Links need to exercise judgment to find a good fit between an Asker's needs and a Giver's resources. When you make a linkage, that reflects on you and affects your relationships with the Giver and Asker. You want to protect both relationships and be careful not to over-use any one Giver.

Most people play all three roles at different times. Being a good Giver and a Link is what allows you to network successfully when it is your turn to be an Asker. The creation and maintenance of an effective network enables individuals and groups to accomplish more in less time, with fewer resources. It is an essential activity for fundraisers.

3

FUNDRAISING TOOLS

Before you bought this book, you probably read the front and back cover to help you decide whether to buy it. Right now, a corporate executive may be reading printed material from your group and deciding whether to donate a few thousand dollars. Electronic communication is growing by leaps and bounds, but print continues to be the most common and practical medium of communication for fundraising.

Printed matter is to a non-profit group what appearance is to the individual. It creates a first impression, it builds an image, it indicates a style, it creates expectations, and it can build interest and curiosity. Whether the presentation will achieve its purpose depends greatly on the quality of the printed material.

Some of your most important tools as a fundraiser are the printed materials your organization produces, and the annual report, objectives sheet, and funding proposal are particularly vital to your efforts. They must be concise, good-looking, and contain essential information. Donations administrators have to deal with many requests from all kinds of groups, and you want to make it easy and pleasant for them to take a look at your group on paper. It is very important that there be no spelling mistakes, typos, or arithmetic errors in these materials. If there are, the potential sponsor can easily say: "If these people can't put out a pamphlet without mistakes, how can we trust them to carry out a $40,000 project successfully?"

In this chapter, you will learn about writing, design, and print production generally and about specific fundraising materials. The emphasis will be on good communication and cost-effectiveness.

a. PRESENTING YOUR ORGANIZATION ON PAPER

As a fundraiser, you need a wide range of skills. One of those skills is presenting your group on paper, in a variety of formats, to a number of different audiences. Nor should your interest in printed material be restricted to fundraising materials, because every piece of paper that goes out of your office represents your group. Try to set an organization-wide standard of quality for printed materials. If possible, all important documents should be typeset and professionally printed. Publications don't need to be flashy or expensive. After all, you don't want sponsors to get the impression you are spending their money to impress them! But they should be clean, neat, attractive, and have a style consistent with your organization.

1. Content and audience

Before beginning any writing project, answer the following important questions:

(a) What do you want to say?

(b) Why do you want to say it?

(c) Whom do you want to reach?

If you don't work out the answers to those questions very carefully, you are already wasting money by pursuing a vague goal. On the other hand, if you can give precise answers to those questions, you will save yourself time, money, and a lot of headaches along the way.

While the first question is pretty easy, the second question, "Why?" often gets an indefinite answer like "to increase public awareness." That's not good enough. Usually you want to provide certain information to motivate people to take a certain action. The question may be easier to answer if it is restated as: "What do you want readers to do after reading your material?" Do you want them to attend an event? Do you want them to give you money? Do you want them to be kinder or more understanding toward a person with a disability? Do you want them to participate in a lobbying effort? Try to be as specific as possible.

Your answer to the third question, "Whom do you want to reach?" may be: "The general public, of course." Wrong. Unless you have the advertising budget of American Express, you had better forget about reaching the general public. The only way a non-profit group can afford to reach the general public is if it deals with an issue newsworthy enough to get free television and newspaper coverage.

Identifying the audience is the toughest part of planning your publication. It requires intuition, experience, and hard-headed thinking. When you are trying to define your audience, consider the following factors:

(a) Age group

(b) Income bracket

(c) Occupation

(d) Cultural background

(e) Lifestyle

(f) Values

(g) Casual interests and hobbies

People who work for non-profit groups tend to be highly motivated, politically aware people with a cause. We are all, in some way, trying to make the world a better place. That's tremendous, so long as you don't forget that your burning cause doesn't even enter into the reality of some others. To reach people, you must try to get inside their minds and understand their life experience, their goals, their concerns.

Try to put yourself in your audience's shoes. You have to find a way to touch their reality, and their reality is different than yours.

Joyce illustrates this briefly with a story from the time she worked at Pollution Probe. "Walking home from work each day, I would see garbage cans overflowing with take-out food containers and think, What a waste of money and resources! I would see cars lined up along the road and think of all the chemicals from those automobile exhausts that were going to be washed into my drinking water. I would see stores filled with consumer goods and wonder how we were going to slow down all this frantic consumption in time to leave some resources for our children. Then I would look at someone near me in the street and know that he or she wasn't seeing any of the things I was seeing. That person was thinking about what to cook for dinner, getting the car fixed, the kids' measles, and just getting by. In order to communicate effectively — in person or in a publication — you must remember that your cause is only one among all the causes and concerns that make up our busy, complex society."

Once those first three questions are answered, you should be able to outline the contents of your publication and decide on a style of writing and a graphic design.

2. Writing

If your publication is not well written, it's not worth the paper it's printed on. A badly written brochure won't be read or understood. The writing should be clear, concise, and direct. Use proper grammar. Avoid jargon; it alienates people who don't understand it. If you must use jargon, define it when it first appears in your text, and spell out acronyms at least once. Sometimes you don't even recognize your own jargon as jargon, so get at least one other person to look over what you've written. Get somebody completely outside your organization to look over your writing and give you a reaction. Any publication that will have broad distribution should be examined by a member of your board of directors *before* it goes to print.

When you've written something, set it aside for at least a day before you go over it again. You will be better able to critique your own writing if you have had a rest from it. If you don't use a computer for writing your first draft, get your work on the word processor before you look at it again. You can be much more objective if you are looking at clean, typed copy.

If you can't write well, hire a freelance writer. If you've answered those first three questions, it shouldn't be difficult or expensive to have a freelance writer pick up your basic idea and do your writing for you.

3. Production

The stages of production are —

(a) choosing a format,

(b) designing a layout,

(c) arranging desktop publishing or typesetting copy,

(d) preparing artwork, and

(e) final computer production.

Once those steps are completed, you have "camera-ready artwork," that is, material ready for the printer.

(a) Format

Format is the shape and size of the publication. It influences communication effectiveness, cost, distribution, and the amount of information the publication can convey.

There are standard formats for brochures, newsletters, annual reports, and books. Size affects the cost of a publication. To keep costs down, select a standard size. Printers buy paper in large sheets and if your publication is in a standard format, such as 8½" x 11", your printer will be able to cut your paper with very little wastage. If you choose an unusual format, there will be paper wastage in the cut, and *you* pay for that wastage.

When choosing format, don't forget to consider the way your publication will be distributed. Will it be posted, handed out, mailed, or displayed? If it is to be mailed, you can save some money with a design and format that can be mailed without an envelope. This is often done with direct mail pieces or newsletters for a large volume mailing. However, postal regulations change often. Before you print, make sure that your design meets the specifications. If you are using an envelope, postal rates may be lower if you use standard size envelopes or smaller envelopes.

Make sure the design fits comfortably in a regular envelope. For example, an $8\frac{1}{2}$" x $5\frac{1}{2}$" booklet will require an odd and unsightly fold to fit into a standard #10 envelope, which is $9\frac{3}{8}$" by $4\frac{1}{8}$". If it is to be displayed, you want to make sure it will fit in the display rack.

You have already defined your audience. Put yourself in their shoes now and ask: "What print formats are *they* familiar with?" Everybody is familiar with newspaper formats. But if you are appealing to potential funders, you may want something more sophisticated, such as an $8\frac{1}{2}$" x 22", two-page spread. The format should always be appropriate for the audience.

(b) Layout

The next step is layout, or your plan of where to put everything in your publication. Layout influences readability, attractiveness, type size, and the amount of information you can fit into your document. In your layout, be sure to break up blocks of type with white space, lines, symbols, graphics, and photographs, if you can use them. The captions under photographs are the first part of the page most people read. Make them interesting. Use them to add to the information conveyed by the photo; don't just repeat the obvious or add names. Put these in boldface, not italics. Type designers find that italics are hard to read if they are more than a few words.

Wall-to-wall type is unattractive and hard to read. If you leave enough white space (areas without type or pictures) in your layout, it will also help break up and balance the inked areas.

(c) Typesetting

We won't go into detail about type sizes and column widths, but we will point out some basics. For readability, 65 characters per line is optimal. To count characters, count the letters, the spaces between words, and all punctuation marks.

Type size, the size of the letters in your publication, is measured in points. This book is set in 11 point type. Column width is measured in picas. Column length is measured in agates. To understand these typesetters' measures, you should buy yourself a ruler marked with points, picas, and agates. Before you go to the typesetter, decide the type size, the typeface, and the column width and mark these clearly on every sheet of copy. For continuity in your publication and to save money, keep the number of different typefaces to a minimum. If you have never worked with typeset copy, get a graphic artist to help you with these decisions. Buying a little expert help is a lot cheaper than having your typesetting done over again. Computer graphic design is harder than it looks. Despite the power of the layout options in modern software, people turn out pages that are often hard to read. Avoid justifying the margins (so that the right margin is an even line) if it leaves rivers of white spaces through your text.

Be sure that you give the typesetter perfect copy. If there are mistakes in the copy, he or she will simply typeset those mistakes. Typesetters are not editors or proofreaders. Your copy should also be typed and perfectly readable; if there are corrections, cross-outs, and scribbled-in additions, the chances are high that the typesetter will make a mistake. Be sure he or she doesn't have to guess at anything.

If you are providing text on a computer disk, or downloading it on a modem, first discuss fonts, formatting symbols, hidden text, and other potential problems with your typesetter or layout artist. "The single biggest problem with text provided on disk," says Frank d'Onofrio of Kwik Kopy in Toronto, "is that groups don't remember to provide the fonts on the disk itself — not descriptions but actual fonts." Talk to your printer first to avoid time and money lost to confusion.

Remember to keep a copy of whatever you give the typesetter, because you should not be charged for corrections made necessary by the typesetter's mistakes. If you have a copy of the material you sent, you can easily determine whether a mistake was yours or the typesetter's. Don't expect your typesetting to be done in one day. Depending on the size of the job and how busy the typesetter is, it could take three days to two weeks to get copy typeset. Have three people proofread the typesetting carefully at least twice each before you sign for it. Don't count on word processing software to check your spelling adequately. It may miss simple errors which substitute the wrong word, spelled correctly, but out of context. For example, a spell checker will not know that you meant to say "She indicated the far manger." NOT "She indicted the fat manager." Any changes that are required after you sign are at your expense.

If this is the first time you have used a typesetter, shop around. You can ask the typesetter for a quotation on a job and you should. Don't go to the typesetter until *all* of your copy is ready because there is usually a minimum charge every time you bring in copy. Headlines are more expensive than body copy.

(d) Artwork

Artwork and graphic design are very much a matter of personal preference, but no matter what your taste, it pays to use an experienced professional. Rates for freelancers vary from $20 per hour to $200 per hour depending on experience and the complexity of the job. Be sure to establish your contractual terms with the artist at the outset:

(a) How much are you going to pay per illustration?

(b) How many illustrations will there be?

(c) Will you be able to see a rough sketch or concept?

(d) If you are going to see finished artwork only, what happens if you don't like it?

Since artwork is a matter of personal taste, it is important to decide who in your group has the ultimate say on production matters. In this situation, decision-making by committee can be a very expensive form of democracy.

(e) Paste-up

If the layout is relatively straightforward, and if you or a person in your organization has a lot of patience and a mind for detail, you can buy the tools or software and do the layout yourself. It is, however, harder than it looks, and crooked paste-up or amateurish computer work can ruin an otherwise good-looking job, so hire a professional if no one else can do it.

4. Printing

Get written quotations from at least three different printers before giving the job to anyone. To estimate the cost, the printer will need the following specifications:

(a) Size

(b) Number of pages

(c) Number of sides to be printed

(d) Quantity

(e) Paper type, weight, recycled content, and colors

(f) Ink types, environmental friendliness and, if you are using colors, how many, and what is required for registration (do they touch or are they close to-gether?)

(g) Bleeds (where the printing goes right to the edge of the page with no margin)

(h) Number of half-tones or screens (photographs specially rendered into dots so they can be printed clearly). The printer will need to know the gradation on the screens, usually a percentage.

(i) Folding

(j) Collating

(k) Binding or stapling

To print your publication, the printer will use different techniques depending on the type of job. For press runs under 10,000 copies, where a single ink color is used, a disposable paper plate is an economical solution.

For longer runs, the printer puts your camera-ready artwork under a large camera and takes a picture of it. This negative is used to make a metal plate. They are ideally suited for jobs requiring higher quality or multi-color printing. The plate is put on the press, the paper and ink are loaded, and your material is printed. This is the photo-offset printing process. Metal plates are slightly more expensive, but are reusable. If you use this technique and think you may need to reprint more copies in future, ask the printer to give the plate to you.

Printing jobs have an economy of scale. The more items you print, the cheaper the unit cost because many of the costs in printing are fixed. Whether you are printing 200 newsletters or 2,000, the printer still has to set up the press.

The major cost variables are the quantity of paper and the time on the press. If your newsletter is in an $8\frac{1}{2}$" x 11" format and your printer has a 17" x 22" press, two newsletters can be printed on each sheet of paper. If the press is 34" x 44", the printer can print three newsletters on each large sheet. The printing is costed in terms of time on the press and the press operator's time. For a run of 10,000 newsletters, you would probably get a more economical job on the larger press.

Black ink is the cheapest. Using a colored ink instead will be a little more expensive because the press has to be washed down, inked in the color you have chosen, and then washed down again after your job is completed. If you are printing in two colors, each sheet has to go through the press twice and that doubles your press time and increases cost. A bleed means that the ink appears to run right over the edge of the page because the margins of the paper are cut off. Bleeds are an additional cost.

There is an infinite range of paper weights, textures, and colors available today. A higher quality paper will hold the ink better and give you a nicer looking job. Brochures are often printed on 50-pound paper, but if you are printing on both sides, you might want to use a heavier stock such as 70-pound paper to reduce see-through. Your printer will show you sample books so that you can select a paper type and weight. You can also select your ink from sample cards. If you select a paper or ink that the printer does not have in stock, it will delay your job.

Folding and collating are pretty straightforward. Your camera-ready artwork should indicate fold-lines.

The cheapest way to bind a 50- to 200-page report is either staple and tape, or cerlox. A booklet would be either saddle-stitched or perfect bound. Saddle-stitch means it is stapled at the fold. This book is perfect bound. Perfect binding is the more expensive of the two, but once you get over 100 pages, saddle-stitch becomes unattractive.

If you don't understand the printing process, you can make some very expensive mistakes, such as publishing a book that loses its pages after the first reading because you skimped on the cost of binding. Funders would not be impressed!

Print production is an art and a science. There is an incredible amount of detail involved and you have to make a lot of decisions along the way. But when you get the package of printed material back from the printer, it's like getting your first check from a new funder. It's all worth it!

b. THE OBJECTIVES SHEET

Your objectives sheet organizes all essential information about your group on one piece of paper. It is a very important document. If you can't afford to print anything else professionally, at least have your objectives sheet printed. Give a good deal of thought to the design and layout. You want a potential funder to be able to look at the objectives sheet for a couple of minutes and get a good overview of your group (see Sample #1).

The core of the objectives sheet is the statement of objectives. We can't over-emphasize the importance of getting this statement right. It tells *why* you are doing what you're doing, not how, or what, or when. That comes later. State your objectives positively and avoid jargon.

You can have more than one objective, but the first one should be all-encompassing. The objective statement should be no longer than a sentence you can read aloud in one breath. Think through every single word and phrase in that statement. Every one counts.

You are writing this for potential donors. If your group is controversial, you have to search for a diplomatic way to state your purpose. Usually, there is some common ground, some area of agreement between what you are working for and what your funders find acceptable.

A gay and lesbian group might state its objective like this: "To foster understanding and tolerance of non-traditional human and sexual relationships."

43

A daycare center might say, "To provide a supervised learning and development situation for children two to five years of age."

A local environmental group might say, "To educate the Jamesborough community about the wise use of our natural resources."

A community legal clinic might say, "To provide a full range of legal advice and services for low-income people in Marysville."

c. ANNUAL REPORT

If your group has been going for less than a year, you won't have published an annual report, but at the end of your first fiscal year, after your financial books have been audited, you should prepare one (see Sample #2).

Next to your objectives sheet, the annual report is your most important fundraising tool. It identifies your group as a business, albeit a non-profit business. All publicly traded corporations and government agencies and some foundations publish annual reports. If you are seeking funds from any financial institution, such as a bank, insurance, or trust company, the first thing it wants to see is your annual report.

When businesses want to check out their competitors or are considering investing in another company, the first thing they look at is that company's annual report. Your group's annual report indicates your businesslike approach. With it, you can present your group in a language and format that corporations and foundations understand and respect.

1. General

If possible, have your annual report professionally designed and printed. It must be neat, well written, and contain the essential information outlined below. If you've never done one before, take a look at the annual reports put out by similar non-profit groups. (They are also a good place to find names

SAMPLE #1
OBJECTIVES SHEET

43 QUEEN'S PARK CRESCENT EAST, TORONTO, ONTARIO M5S 2C3

THE POLLUTION PROBE FOUNDATION

OBJECTIVES: 1976-77

To promote and demonstrate the conserver society ethic.

To be the catalyst for involving business, government and the public in environmental improvement.

To advocate wise management of agricultural land resources.

To continue to promote environmental education in Ontario schools.

To encourage the adoption of provincial and national energy policies with an emphasis on energy conservation and renewable energy.

To demonstrate the environmental and economic soundness of renewable energy in Canada.

Within this frame work the Pollution Probe Foundation is undertaking the following two projects.

POLLUTION PROBE
PROGRAM 1976-77

LAND MANAGEMENT:

We will form a coalition for preservation of agricultural land in Ontario. Specifically, we will join with local environmental groups to protect the 7,000 acres of Niagara farmland threatened by the Niagara Regional Council's plan to expand urban boundaries.-

CONSERVER EDUCATION:

We will alert the public to environmentally damaging consumer products and wasteful packaging.

We will design a "Do-It" poster, to help individuals maintain and improve their personal environments.

We will continue to respond to over 500 information requests per week from the public.

We will provide teachers with current information on our special areas of concentration, including: The Noise Kit, Family Ecology, Art and the Environment, Literature and the Environment, and guides to 20 environmental tours in Metro Toronto.-

FOOD RESEARCH:

We will develop a campaign for safer, more nutritious food.

We will study the effect on public health of the industrialization of food production.

NOTE: We will maintain an organizational flexibility so that we can respond to urgent environmental problems as they arise.

ENERGY PROBE / A PROJECT OF THE POLLUTION PROBE FOUNDATION

PROGRAM: 1976-77

NATIONAL ENERGY POLICY

We will continue an active role in the Mackenzie Valley Pipeline debate by making our case before the National Energy Board. We will comment on national energy issues such as oil supply and off-shore oil drilling.

RENEWABLE ENERGY

We will continue our Canada-wide campaign on renewable energy by:
Continuing distribution of our Renewable Energy Handbook.
Urging the manufacture and marketing of renewable energy technologies in Canada.
We will demonstrate the practicability of environmentally appropriate technologies by undertaking a 2 year ECO HOUSE PROJECT in downtown Toronto which incorporates solar heating systems, energy conservation measures and alternative waste disposal.

ROYAL COMMISSION ON ELECTRICAL POWER PLANNING

At the "Porter Commission" Energy Probe will advocate a mixed energy economy based on energy conservation and matching of energy sources to their 'end use'. Through the commission's public interest office, we will assist other citizens' groups who wish to participate.

CANDU II

More than 100 nuclear reactors are planned for Canada by the year 2000. Our second publication on the Canadian nuclear system, will scrutinize the economic, social and environmental impact of nuclear energy. CANDU II will inform government and corporate decision-makers, and concerned individuals of our viewpoint on nuclear energy.

FUNDING

Probe's yearly budget is met by donations and grants from individuals, corporations, government and foundations.
The Pollution Probe Foundation is a Registered Charitable Organization (Reg. No.   ) and donations are tax deductible.
Probe's accounts are prepared under the supervision of Price Waterhouse and Company.

FUNDING OBJECTIVES for the year

Pollution Probe at the University of Toronto	$ 55,800
Energy Probe	$ 80,000
Program Research and Administration	$ 20,300
Fundraising	$ 22,500
Total	$178,600

Telephone Numbers
Pollution Probe   978-7152   Administration 978-6477
Energy Probe   978-7014   Fundraising   978-6319
ADDRESS: 43 Queen's Park Crescent East, Toronto, Ontario M5S 2C3

of potential funders!) To a large extent, corporations and foundations are going to judge your group on the basis of this one document. So put due time, thought, and, if you have it, money, into the annual report.

Try to get the annual report out as soon as possible after your year-end. You can't print it until you have the auditor's report, but you can get it ready for printing.

The length of your annual report will depend on the size of your group and how many activities you have to describe. For small groups, a one-page, two-fold pamphlet will do the job. Large groups will need a small booklet to convey the information. Keep it concise and stick to basic, essential information.

2. Essential elements of an annual report

(a) Financial statement

The financial statement is the real reason behind an annual report. Hand your annual report to a corporate president and he or she will turn straight to the financial statement. If your group's annual income is $50,000 or more, you should have an annual audit stating your income, expenditures, and balance at the year-end. The auditor's report will be printed in your annual report.

The potential sponsor wants to get an idea of your financial size and management. Before giving you money, he or she wants some proof that you know how to manage money wisely. Balance sheets don't tell lies.

If you have a deficit, be prepared to explain to a potential donor why you have it and how you intend to get out of it. Look at your deficit and calculate it as a percentage of your annual income. A deficit greater than 5% of your annual income will look particularly bad. It might be useful to have your bookkeeper do a rough balance sheet a few months before your year-end, so that you can get an idea of the size

47

of the deficit and decide if there are any emergency measures that can be taken.

If you have a running deficit, the balance sheet will show what it was at your present year-end and what it was the year before that. It's very bad to have a deficit in the first place, and if that deficit is growing every year, it's worse! That tells a potential sponsor that you aren't a good money manager. If your deficit keeps growing, your sponsors are going to decide that they are throwing money away by funding you, and they are going to say NO.

One group that was facing a deficit at year-end asked staff to forego salary for one month in order to clear the deficit on the books. So, in effect, the staff actually paid the debt. It was a drastic measure that hurt in the short term, but it managed to put the group in a much better position to raise funds in the coming year. Groups that are in the red make sponsors nervous.

(b) Activities and achievements

Point out the impact you had on your community in the past year. You want to impress your readers by presenting a positive past and a rosy future. Specifically, you should answer the following questions:

(a) What did you do last year? You could cite conferences, policy papers, research, campaigns, publications, or services for example.

(b) How many people did you serve? Mention telephone and written inquiries, and speaking engagements, if applicable.

(c) What did you achieve? Be as specific as possible, but don't be afraid to brag a little. If you are lobbying for certain changes in legislation or social attitudes, indicate what progress you have made. Philosophize a little.

If you are a service group, running a daycare or a half-way house or assisting disabled children, for example, you will want to put more emphasis on activities and on the number of people your group served in its different capacities. Paint a picture of what your service meant to these people. Include photographs or quotations that support your points. Point out that you provided this service economically.

If you are an issue group, you may be able to point out that you played a role in achieving some concrete changes. But don't make claims to fame that you can't back up.

(c) History

Write a few paragraphs about when your group was formed, what its purpose is, where you've come from, where you're at, and where you're heading.

(d) Sponsors

List all corporations, foundations, and government agencies that funded your group during the fiscal year unless they indicate that their contributions are to be anonymous. Be sure to spell their names correctly and exactly the way they have it on their letterhead. (The same practice should be applied in your correspondence with them.) Don't forget anybody! Don't indicate how much they gave, just who gave. List them alphabetically.

Companies who gave you their services for free or at cost, such as the accounting or legal firm you use, and companies who gave free envelopes, paper, or whatever, should also be listed as donors. The more sponsors you can justifiably list, the better your group will look, and this is one of the best ways to acknowledge donors' contributions.

(e) Board of directors

List the full names of the people on your board, and, if the members will let you, where they work, or other relevant positions they hold.

(f) Staff

Be sure that you also include the executive director's and the fundraiser's name and phone number. You should also remember to provide the organization's full address on the annual report. You can list names, phone numbers, and titles of permanent staff if you like.

3. Distribution

Send your annual report to all corporations, foundations, and government sources you *approached* for funding in the past year, not just those who gave you money. Send it to the corporations and foundations you plan to approach next year. Any individuals who gave you a large sum of money ($100 or more), should also receive a copy of your annual report. Send it to key volunteers, elected officials (if you want government funding), the people you serve (if you want them to feel like equal partners), and staff (if you want them well-informed.)

You should send it to your local media as well: it may help you to get valuable press coverage. Media attention contributes to a high profile, which translates into successful fundraising.

In the United States, send your annual report to the Foundation Center's cooperating collection in the city or state where your group operates.

In Canada, send it to The Canadian Centre for Business and the Community (formerly known as The Institute of Donations and Public Affairs Research). The Centre is a non-profit organization affiliated with The Conference Board of Canada. It provides objective information and analysis in the

50

area of corporate community investment. It is set up to serve corporate donors, not charities. They do not match non-profit groups with donors. However, they want to have background data handy, just in case the companies ask for verification.

The Centre now has four components: Corporate Community Investment Policy and Practices; Community Economic Development; Partnerships and Alliances; and Corporate Social Responsibility and Ethics.

George Khoury, the Centre's Director, told *Front and Centre* magazine (the newspaper of The Canadian Centre for Philanthropy, 1329 Bay Street, Toronto, Ontario. See July 1995 issue) that the move reflects a changing relationship between corporations and communities. "Donations aren't the only way of supporting communities," he says. "There's a move toward a more strategic approach, to supporting communities on a more sustainable basis through community development projects."

The Centre recommends that any group launching a corporate donations request send information about themselves to the Centre's *nearest* office (*not* to all of them). See the following addresses:

714 - 1st Street SE
3rd Floor
Calgary, AB
T2G 2G8
Tel: (403) 233-0720
Fax: (403) 262-3436

255 Smyth Road
Ottawa, ON
K1H 8M7
Tel: (613) 526-3280
Fax: (613) 526-4857

55 University Avenue
Suite 1800
Toronto, ON
M5J 2H7
Tel: (416) 360-2372
Fax: (416) 360-2905

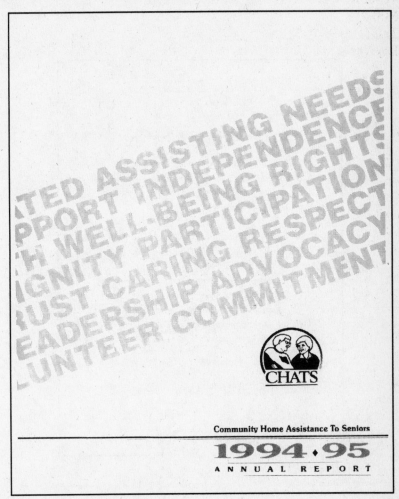

* Reprinted with permission by CHATS (Community Home Assistance to Seniors)

The CHATS Mission

CHATS is dedicated to assisting seniors with the everyday needs of community living in support of personal independence, good health and well-being.

CHATS believes in:
♦ The client's right to choice, dignity and independence
♦ Promoting community participation
♦ Building trust, caring and respect
♦ Innovative leadership and advocacy
♦ Developing staff and volunteer commitment

from the **CHATS** board of directors

1994/1995 Strategic Directions

1. To carry forward the CHATS mission into the design of the Multi-Service Agency model.

2. To plan in partnership with related agencies.

3. To position strengths of CHATS for maximum contribution to system reform.
   - community connections and participation
   - wellness model of care co-ordination
   - specialization of services to meet the needs of the frail elderly

Board of Directors, from left to right, back row: Joe Nightwander, Leonore Graham; Sarah Stapleton; Bonnie Linkletter; Bob Harvey, Treasurer.
Front row, left to right: Nance Harris; Dorothy Gilbert; Barbara Caiger, Chairperson; Lois Cormack.
Missing from picture: Lynelle Hamilton; Irwin Peters; Anne Fillett, Past Chair.

. . . in support of personal independence, good health and well-being
of seniors . . .

SAMPLE #2 — Continued

Making a Difference

In my experience, when a monumental task looms, people throw up their hands and ask what difference they could make in the whole scheme of things. The massive task of system reform of Long Term Care in York Region, could easily have elicited that tack. Fortunately that is not the case. The Long Term Care Division Area Office and The District Health Council have provided opportunities for people to become involved.

MSA Plans – Promoting the CHATS Mission

A year ago, the CHATS Board of Directors reaffirmed its support of the District Health Council in the development of a Multi Service Agency (MSA) in York Region. Our strategic plan is to carry forward the CHATS mission to this agency; seeking opportunities for partnership and focus on the excellent quality of service to the frail elderly in York Region.

CAP – Promoting Responsive Services

In our work with Community Agencies in Partnership (CAP) we are encouraging breaking down barriers and creating a seamless service. To pursue our strategy for partnership we have:

♦ collaborated with other agencies to initiate the 1-800 Access Project

♦ initiated a joint proposal to the Ministry of Health for funding a cost analysis of the present system

♦ with others, planned the Quick Response System, streamlining services following hospital discharge.

New Directions – Providing Service Excellence

In a recent significant decision, the CHATS' Board recognized the need for a fund raising and public relations plan, to continue to provide excellent service to our clients while the Long Term Care Reform plans unfold. Recognizing the limitations of government assisted services, we support a greater emphasis on volunteer programs. In keeping with our strategy, we will be looking for new opportunities for collaboration in these areas.

While the Board policy on interim management limits expansion of service, an opportunity to enhance the Respite Program caused us to rethink this for individual issues. Providing subsidy to care givers for this service made the expansion conducive to our overall objectives.

Over the past year, the Board has been somewhat frustrated in the protracted process of long term care reform. We want to work, with the District Health Council and other agencies, to provide a better, cost effective and more responsive service to people in York Region.

As we move into our fifteenth year of operation, the Board is proud of the service of our competent and caring staff and volunteers. We recognize the difference CHATS makes to the frail elderly in our community. We continue to support linkages with other organizations and agencies to enhance and improve services. We celebrate the successes and congratulate all who make CHATS an integral part of caring for the frail elderly in York Region.

As I complete my term as Chair of the Board of Directors, I feel positive about our direction. I am grateful for all the support I have received and for the opportunity to serve in an organization that is making a difference.

3

. . . the client's right to choice, dignity and independence . . .

Embracing the Challenge of Change

Board-stated Strategic Directions and Program Strategies guided operations over the past year. Admittedly, our focus was somewhat swayed by the necessity to manage a 40% increase in our homemaking services alone. Some highlights follow to give you an insight on our priorities.

Developing a Client-Focused Structure

Organizational re-structuring reflects our commitment to decentralized management and services at a local community level. We have emphasized the support role of CHATS' Administration Office to the Branches and increased our emphasis on Branch teams able to work together to meet unique local service needs.

Partnerships to Meet Client Needs

The Quick Response Service in York Region is CHATS' first joint venture with local hospitals and other community service providers. Hospital admissions now can be avoided with appropriate, immediate, support provided through CHATS' homemaking service and partner agencies.

A 1-800 information hotline was established with York Region community agencies for seniors, family caregivers and people with physical disabilities.

These are tentative beginnings to more substantial work required for a better integrated and more efficient long term care system.

Increasing Community Participation

We are excited about the review, enhancement and expansion of our volunteer services for next year – particularly Meals on Wheels, Friendly Visiting and Lunch Out – with increased support from community fundraising. The groundwork was laid by our commitment to upgrading volunteer management and emphasis on community development. Our comprehensive evaluation of the Meals on Wheels Program, to be completed shortly, will be the first service area to launch our future direction.

Supporting the Needs of Caregivers

Raising the profile of our Caregiver Relief Program and eliminating some barriers to service will be launched with the recent approval for enhancement funding from the Provincial Government.

Managing the Budget Challenge

Our financial position is stable, finishing the year with a small surplus. General fundraising of $63,000 exceeded our target by $10,000. Homemaker orientation and in-service training, the foundation for quality service, earmarks the surplus funds as we are regrettably unable to finance these costs through our base budget. Computerization of Branch offices is a priority for project funding in 1995/96 allowing Branch staff to efficiently deliver services.

I thank the many contributors to CHATS' success in the past year: the Board members, staff, volunteers, partner agencies, community donors and our funders. As we approach our 15th anniversary year, we honour our beginnings with an ever-present focus on CHATS Mission and Values which has brought us to where we are today . . . and will continue to lead us into the future!

. . . Building trust, caring and respect . . .

Branch Highlights

Bonjourno!

The West Branch developed an Italian dictionary and tape to assist Homemakers with Italian speaking clients.

Staff Resource

Branch offices expanded office volunteer recruitment and student placements from community college gerontology programs this year.

CHATS Volunteer Honoured

Longtime East Branch volunteer, Marion Damude, received an award in recognition of her outstanding involvement with CHATS as Lunch Out Coordinator. York Region Healthy Communities Coalition made the presentation.

Training Partners

Markham Stouffville Hospital supported volunteer training at the East Branch with facility space and instruction from their physiotherapy staff.

Volunteer Recognition

More than 400 volunteers participated in special recognition events this year.

Support From the Community

The North Branch Lunch Out Program depends solely on local restaurants, churches, high schools, the Historical Society, retirement lodges, local entertainers and service clubs for its continued success.

Hospice Georgina

The week of April 24th was declared Hospice Week in Georgina. Volunteers distributed literature and buttons from displays in shopping areas. Articles appeared in the local newspapers; a film was aired on local Cable TV; letters were sent to all physicians, service clubs and agencies; and personal presentations were made to several service clubs.

Service Involvement from Business

The Royal Bank continues to provide time for their staff members who volunteer for the CHATS Meals on Wheels Program, delivering noontime meals for our clients.

CHATS
5

Mr. Leslie Taylor, a CHATS North Branch client, a recipient of Homemaking, Friendly Visiting, and Meals on Wheels, is thrown a 94th surprise birthday party at the home of Fran Palmer (one of his Homemakers). In attendance were (L to R) VON Nurse Linda Rapos, CHATS Homemakers Ellen Friedwold & Fran Palmer, CHATS Friendly Visitor Cassie Doherty and CHATS Sutton Homemaker Team Leader, Chris Owen.

. . . Promoting community participation . . .

Provincial, Regional & Local Involvements

Community Agencies in Partnership
- Collaborating at a Board and staff level with York Region community agencies on the delivery of long term care services.

Ontario Community Support Association
- Contributing to the development of standardized training for Homemaker Supervisors and new training standards for Homemakers through the Personal Support Worker Project.
- Influencing the Provincial Government's Long Term Care policy direction.
- Advocating for homemaking program issues with the Long Term Care Division of the Ministry of Health.

York Region District Health Council
- Contributing to the planning and future direction of the Long Term Care system in York Region.

York Region Human Services Computer Network
- Exploring the potential for computer networking between organizations.

Ontario Association of Volunteer Administrators
- Supporting provincial professional development standards and practices for volunteer management.

Council on Aging
- Participating as a member to support advocacy of seniors issues with seniors and related organizations in York Region.

Other Involvements Contributing to Service Integration and Co-ordination
- 1-800 Access Project
- Quick Response Service Project
- York Region Homemaker Advisory Committee & Working Group
- York Region Elder Abuse Committee
- Alzheimers Society Advisory Committee
- Transportation Advocacy Network, Community Services Council
- Tenant Support Services Project, York Region Housing Authority
- Placement Co-ordination Service Advisory Committee
- Falls and the Elderly Project, York Region Public Health
- Metropolitan Toronto Inter-agency Meals on Wheels Committee
- York Region Multicultural Network

Speaking of leadership . . . some East Branch personnel posed for an informal shot . . . pictured from left to right: Sue Higginson, Sue Boyd, Peggy Law, Sharron Reagan, Joanne Cameron, and Kathy White.

. . . innovative leadership and advocacy . . .

CHATS
6

Key Initiatives to Support Service Quality

Meals on Wheels Evaluation

A Meals on Wheels Program Evaluation was conducted during the past year. The purpose being to collect information from a variety of sources to assist CHATS in further developing the program to be responsive to community needs, while streamlining the program to be as effective and efficient as possible. Final report to be available in June.

Service Co-ordinator Training Project

The Ontario Community Support Association developed training for Service Co-ordinators with funding from the Trillium Foundation. This training was developed in response to issues identified by agencies delivering Home-making and Home Support Services. It focuses on areas of leadership, communication, legislation, quality management, problem solving, teambuilding, enabling behaviours and administration. We are very pleased to participate in this training and appreciate the benefit to both staff and clients.

Personal Support Worker Training Project

A new training program has been developed for Homemakers, Home Support Workers, Health Care Aids and Personal Attendants. This program is designed to assist the worker to meet the increasing challenges anticipated in the community as our population ages. It takes into account the workers' prior learning, offers a variety of exit points, provides for advanced learning in specialized areas and offers opportunity for advancement.

We are excited about this program and anxiously await approval of the Ministry of Health and the Ministry of Education and Training.

Staff Compensation

A Compensation Plan was developed to meet pay equity requirements. A longer term compensation strategy is working towards equitable compensation levels to support the recruitment and retention of quality staff.

Qualified Homemakers Available

At the end of this year, 88% of CHATS Home-makers have completed community college training at the Level II designation or equivalent. With targeted hiring and a volunteer on-call roster, Homemakers are available for service on evenings, weekends, overnights and on-call. Mileage and travel time policies were revised to support clients who need evening "tuck-in" service.

Palliative Care Training

Homemakers and Service Co-ordinators participated in palliative care training modules including: core concepts, advanced issues in palliative care and train the trainer.

Homemaker Administration Time

Administration time was re-directed to increase one-on-one supervision and small group discussions focused on client care issues in addition to regular staff meetings.

Laura Taylor, 87, East Branch client – another QRS success story!

... developing staff and volunteer commitment ...

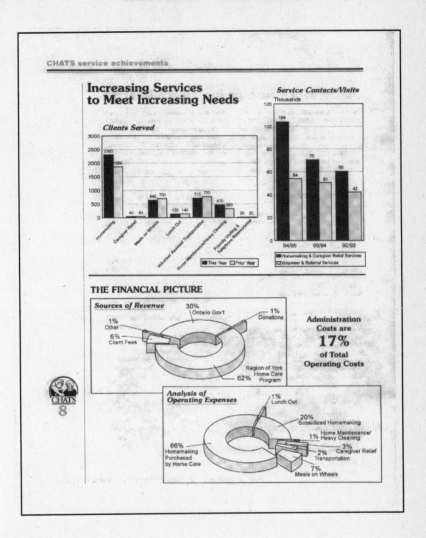

CHATS service achievements

Increasing Services to Meet Increasing Needs

Clients Served

Service Contacts/Visits
Thousands

THE FINANCIAL PICTURE

Sources of Revenue

Administration Costs are **17%** of Total Operating Costs

Analysis of Operating Expenses

CHATS service achievements

Service Statistics

		94/95	93/94	
Homemaking Program: Assists with personal care and household management	Hours:	214,100	153,000	40% SERVICE GROWTH
Caregiver Relief Program: Provides relief from caregiving responsibilities for families	Hours:	3,245	4,600	TARGETTED FOR EXPANSION
Meals on Wheels: Provides a noon-time meal delivered at home with the reassurance of a volunteer contact	Meals:	34,600	35,500	EVALUATION RESULTS SOON
Lunch Out Program: Provides a noon-time meal in a social setting	Meals:	1,050	1,050	
Volunteer-Assisted Transportation: Trips for medical, shopping and other needs	Trips:	7,900	6,900	
Home Maintenance /Heavy Cleaning: Referrals to screened providers assist with basic household needs	Hours:	3,200	2,500	
Friendly Visiting and Telephone Reassurance Programs: Reach out to isolated seniors	Visits:	1,950	2,100	TARGETTED FOR EXPANSION
Information & Referral Services: Help make connections to other services	Enquiries:	2,700	2,400	RE-DIRECT CALLS TO NEW 1-800 #

CHATS
9

	94/95	93/94	
Hours of Volunteer Service	20,100	18,150	
Number of Volunteers Active this Year	880	730	+ 20% Volunteers
Total Number of Staff	276	209	
Number of Homemakers	232	174	
Members of Other Staff	44	35	

62

CHATS - Community Home Assistance to Seniors
[operated by Home Support Services for York Region]

Financial Highlights

AUDITORS' REPORT

We have examined the financial statements of **CHATS - Community Home Assistance to Seniors** [operated by Home Support Services for York Region] and have reported thereon to the Board of Directors on May 5, 1995. Our examination included the accompanying condensed balance sheet, condensed statement of operations and reserve fund and was made in accordance with generally accepted auditing standards.

In our opinion, the accompanying condensed financial statements fairly summarize the related information contained in the financial statements examined by us.

Ernst + Young

Thornhill, Canada,
May 5, 1995.

Chartered Accountants

≡II *ERNST & YOUNG*

CHATS - Community Home Assistance to Seniors
[operated by Home Support Services for York Region]

Financial Highlights

CONDENSED BALANCE SHEET

As at March 31

	1995 $	1994 $
ASSETS		
Current		
Cash	74,814	39,083
Accounts receivable	444,621	393,077
Grants receivable	—	154,423
Other	37,986	17,297
	556,621	603,880
LIABILITIES AND EQUITY		
Current		
Accounts payable and accrued liabilities	192,160	300,183
Equity		
Designated funds	125,481	192,273
Reserve fund	238,980	111,424
Total equity	364,461	303,697
	556,621	603,880

CONDENSED STATEMENT OF OPERATIONS AND RESERVE FUND

Year ended March 31

	1995 $	1994 $
Revenue		
Home Care and client fees	3,673,692	2,360,309
Ministry of Health, operating subsidy and grants	1,612,210	1,660,957
Donations	72,046	48,422
Other grants	15,657	—
Other	11,809	13,954
	5,385,414	4,083,642
Expenses		
Salaries, wages and employee benefits	4,497,115	3,715,427
Office operations	361,496	264,442
Other	308,087	207,042
Food costs	157,952	164,519
	5,324,650	4,351,430
Excess (deficiency) of revenue over expenses before the undernoted	60,764	(267,788)
Net transfers from designated funds	66,792	267,788
Excess of revenue over expenses for the year	127,556	—
Reserve fund, beginning of year	111,424	111,424
Reserve fund, end of year	238,980	111,424

Complete audited financial statements are available upon request.

CHATS
11

64

Board of Directors

Barbara Caiger, Chairperson
Joe Nighswander, Vice-Chair
Irwin Peters, Second Vice-Chair
Bob Harvey, Treasurer
Lynelle Hamilton, Past Chair
Dorothy Gilbert
Sarah Stapleton
Anne Filleti
Lois Cormack
Bonnie Linkletter
Leonore Graham
Nance Harris

Finance Committee

Bob Harvey, Chairperson
Betty Walsh
Wayne MacDougall
Trent Tunstall
Kim MacDonald

Community Relations & Fund Development Committee

Sharon Neally, Chairperson
Frank Findlay
Bonnie Linkletter

Meals on Wheels Committee

Dorothy Gilbert, Chairperson
Nancy Wright, Vice-Chair
Faye Fretz, Second Vice-Chair
Margaret Baldassare
Joan Davenport
Jean Flooryp
Joanne Franzese
Mollie Froud
Janice Gervais
Audrey Gibson
Audrey Jones
Claire MacAlpine
Marilyn Oldfield
June Ponting
Annemarie Powell
Mary Queen
Ilse Thompson

CHATS
12

Did you know . . .

73% of clients live alone
56% of clients are over 80 years of age
10% of clients are over 90 years of age

More than 3,000 seniors were assisted by CHATS this year.

Almost 50% of our clients are requiring help with 2 or more services to support their independence.

CHATS Gratefully Acknowledges
the generous gifts of money, goods and services
from our community supporters

Government

Long Term Care Division, Ministry of Health
York Region Home Care Program
Region of York Social Services Division

Businesses

Angus Restaurant
Alexander Muir Retirement Home
AMP Markham
All Seasons Party Rentals
Anchor Restaurant
Bank of Montreal
Beckers Funeral Home*
Becky's Own Original Designs
Bell Canada, Realty Services
Beres Tire Centre
Burrows Medical
Canadian Imperial Bank of Commerce
Cansoto Systems Inc.
Cartwright Foundation
Cedarvale Lodge
Cook's Bay Marina
D.L. Copplestone Office Furnishing
Crayola
Deemac Furniture
Eaglewood
Etherington Insurance*
Fancy Stamp Printing*
Flowers by Marilyn
Flowers Fantasia
Food Save
Glenway Country Club
Granite Restaurant
Greensacres
Growers Direct
Helen Florist
High Tech Communications
IBM
Impact Business Systems
Johnson's Marina
Laird & Laird Insurance Brokers*
Madsen's Greenhouses
Peninsula Restaurant
Priority Courier
Proctor & Gamble
Royal Bank of Canada
Seneca College
Sunkist Food Market, Richmond Hill
Sutton District High School Choir
Taylor Funeral Home, Keswick*
Sutton Foodland
Sutton Pantry
Watersfield Gallery
Venner Woodworking
York County Physiotherapy & Sports Injuries Clinic

Service Clubs/Community Groups

4th Unionville Brownies
13th Markham Brownies
Beavers
Bethavan Women's Institute, Keswick
Brownies
Cedarcrest Manor
Elder Mills, Women's Institute, Woodbridge
Girl Guides
King City Lions Club
Keswick Lioness Club
Kinette Club, Newmarket
Kiwanis Club, Unionville
Kleinburg Seniors
Knights of Columbus, Richmond Hill
Lake Simcoe Lady Crafters
Loyal Orange Lodge, Sutton
Maples of Ballantrae
Markham-Stouffville Hospital
McConaghy Centre
Newmarket Veterans Association
North 39ers Seniors Club, Sutton
Order of the Eastern Star, Chapter 282, Newmarket
Order of the Eastern Star, Chapter 356, Richmond Hill
Pefferlaw Lioness Club
Richmond Hill Curling Club/Day Ladies Section
Richmond Hill Lions Club
Richvale Lions Club
Royal Canadian Legion, Br 385, Aurora
Royal Canadian Legion, Br 375, Richmond Hill
Royal Canadian Legion, Br 356, Sutton
Royal Canadian Legion, Br 414, Woodbridge
Stouffville Lions Club
Stouffville Silver Jubilee Club
Stouffville Progress Club
Thornhill Community Centre
Thornhill District Lions Club
Vaughan Information

Churches

Aurora United Church
Bahais of Newmarket
Baptist Church, Women, Newmarket
Church of the Nazarene
Holy Trinity Church, Thornhill
Keswick United Church
Knox United Church
Ravenshoe United Church (Women)
St Andrews Presbyterian Church
St. Patrick's Women's Auxiliary, Markham
Trinity United Church
United Church Women, Keswick
Woodbridge United Church

Designated contributions to Hospice Georgina

CHATS gratefully acknowledges

Northlands Printing
and
VILLAGE GRAPHICS & COMMUNICATIONS
274 Cedarholme Ave , Keswick, Ontario L4P 9M5

for partial funding of the 1994/95 Annual Report

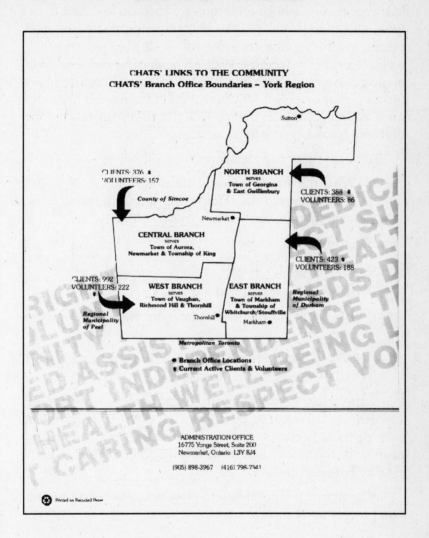

CHATS' LINKS TO THE COMMUNITY
CHATS' Branch Office Boundaries – York Region

Sutton

CLIENTS: 376 ✱
VOLUNTEERS: 157

NORTH BRANCH
serves
Town of Georgina
& East Gwillimbury

CLIENTS: 388 ✱
VOLUNTEERS: 86

County of Simcoe

Newmarket ●

CENTRAL BRANCH
serves
Town of Aurora,
Newmarket & Township of King

CLIENTS: 423 ✱
VOLUNTEERS: 188

CLIENTS: 992 ✱
VOLUNTEERS: 222
✱

WEST BRANCH
serves
Town of Vaughan,
Richmond Hill & Thornhill

EAST BRANCH
serves
Town of Markham
& Township of
Whitchurch/Stouffville

*Regional
Municipality
of Durham*

*Regional
Municipality
of Peel*

Thornhill ●

Markham ●

Metropolitan Toronto

● Branch Office Locations
✱ Current Active Clients & Volunteers

ADMINISTRATION OFFICE
16775 Yonge Street, Suite 200
Newmarket, Ontario L3Y 8J4

(905) 898-3967   (416) 798-7341

Printed on Recycled Paper

67

d. FUNDING PROPOSAL

Many projects are born on impulse, raised on love and over-time, and then join the ranks of other unpublished master-pieces. Why? Because they weren't well planned and they weren't properly funded. Writing a funding proposal will help you overcome both hurdles: to write a successful project funding proposal, you will have to plan the project first, and once your proposal is completed, it will aid in raising the dollars to make your project a success.

To begin planning, determine the following:

(a) Why the project should be done. (Prove it hasn't already been done.) Help the donor understand what societal problem you are trying to fix.

(b) How it will be done

(c) How long it will take

(d) How much it will cost

(e) Who will do the work and why they are the right people

(f) What end product or impact will result and how it will be measured and evaluated

In the actual proposal, these components are given more sophisticated names. A description of what is required in each of these sections follows. If you have not done many proposals, try to look at a few done by other groups in your locality before you start.

When your proposal is complete and ready to present, don't forget to include a covering letter.

1. Introduction and rationale (Why?)

State the project's objective and define the need for this project in concrete and meaningful terms. You may know the project is needed — but you have to define and describe that need well enough to convince someone else it's needed. The staff of issue-oriented groups tend to be so committed to their cause that they don't have a realistic perspective on it. What you do may well seem obscure and irrelevant to most people. The key to writing a convincing rationale is to put your issue in perspective with other social issues, and to show why and how it affects many people.

Explain why your group is best-suited to do the project. Outline your previous interest and accomplishments in this field.

This section of your proposal is vital because if your introduction and rationale are not convincing, a funder won't read any further. Try to excite an interest; write an up-beat, appealing rationale. Avoid jargon if possible; if you must use it — define it. Watch your assumptions.

2. Project description (How?)

How will you accomplish your objective? How will you fill the need you have defined? How are you going to provide the needed information or service?

Be specific. For example, if you proposed to write and produce a booklet, this section would include a table of contents. If it is being printed — will you use photocopies, dot matrix, laser printer quality, or offset printing? How many illustrations and how many pages will there be? What is the size of the pages? You need to make these kinds of decisions in order to budget accurately, so indicate them in this section. It will prove that you know what you're doing.

3. Schedule (How long?)

Break the project down into phases and indicate how long each will take. For the booklet example above, you might present a time schedule for each of research, writing and editing, printing, promotion, and distribution. Show the schedule in numbers of weeks or months. Don't say, "Research: January to March." Say, "Research: three months." You never know how long it will take to fund the project, so you don't know exactly when you will be able to put your schedule into effect.

4. Budget (How much?)

Budgeting is a science — a science that intimidates many people. The biggest challenge is to budget accurately, and that requires research, unless you are familiar with current prices.

Some fundraisers play a silly game of "Ask for twice as much as you need because they will only give you half of what you ask for." If that is your attitude, you underestimate the intelligence of the person who will evaluate your proposal. Funding administrators can spot a padded budget at a glance. You will lose credibility and respect if you pad budgets. Joyce once saw a project budget that required an aerial survey. It happened that the plane was owned and operated by the project coordinator. Plane rental was budgeted at $200 an hour. Commercial rental of a private plane with pilot then cost about $80 an hour. The funder requested an adjustment for this item.

Since you will be providing a staff profile in the proposal, make sure that the staff salaries you list are consistent with staff qualifications. Assign a figure that is near market value for that person's skills.

It's important that the cost of a project be reasonable and realistic. Step back and take a long, hard look at the cost in relation to the project and the issue. That's exactly what a potential funder is going to do and, unless it looks sensible, he or she is not going to fund you. For some types of projects you can gauge this by calculating a unit cost. For example, if a writing, research, and publishing project has a total budget of $20,000 and you print 500 books, the cost per book is $40. If you print 2,000 books, the cost per book is $10. Similarly, a service group could calculate the cost per client served. Is it a reasonable cost compared to other groups?

Be sure to include *all* project costs in your budget. Postage, fax transmissions, courier service, computer time, and long distance telephone calls are often forgotten. It is acceptable to include an item called "contingency" which can be no greater than 10% of your total budget. The contingency money will take care of unforeseen and unavoidable cost over-runs. Budget salary time for project supervision and management. This takes a good deal of time, and it's a necessary part of the project, so budget for it.

Printing costs are difficult to budget. Once you make the decisions on size, format, and number of copies, phone a few printers and get estimates. If the project is over $5,000, include a written estimate from a printer in the proposal appendix. (When you do the job you should get bids from three different printers.)

A proposal with a budget of $30,000 or more should also include a bookkeeping or auditing fee. Government agencies and many foundations require detailed accounting for grants.

Sample #3 is an example of a budget for the writing, production, and distribution of a short book. The book will be 7" x 9" (18 cm x 23 cm), 60 pages long, typeset, and printed on an offset press. Five hundred copies will be printed. This sample is presented to illustrate budget format and detail. The prices are meaningful but not intended to be 100% accurate.

5.   Personnel (Who?)

The annual report will indicate your group's previous experience and interest in this field and your charitable registration number. Letters of support are helpful, but make sure that they are directly relevant to the specific project. If you are approaching a government source, a letter from your mayor, governor, or member of parliament is valuable. If your group or project is controversial, a letter of endorsement from a respected authority in the field will lend credibility.

Include a staff profile of the person(s) who will carry out the project, giving the name, education, and relevant experience. You need to convince prospective donors that you have the personnel to successfully complete the job. Only list those staff and volunteers who will be directly involved in the project. Also list all board members and what credentials, skills, or experience they bring to this project.

6. Anticipated results (What?)

Describe the project's end-product. How many people will benefit and how? What will you have to show for the time and money invested? What changes in public awareness, data base, legislation, or services can be expected? Be as specific as possible. Quantify your results. You are explaining how you are going to evaluate the project once it is completed. Funders have no way to evaluate their contribution or your success unless you evaluate the project. By doing this, you are setting a goal and making a commitment to sponsors. It should be realistic and achievable, but should be significant enough to justify the financial investment. This section should answer the toughest question a funder can ask: "So what?"

Funders increasingly demand a rigorous evaluation process. If, for example, the project involves printing a booklet, they want to know not only that you printed it, but also how you plan to find out if people actually read it. If people do read it, the funders want to know how you plan to find out if it had any impact on them. They want to know what lessons your group expects to learn from this project, and how you will share them with other groups.

Sample #4 is an actual project funding proposal prepared by the Canadian Environmental Law Research Foundation. The proposal contains the essential parts of a proposal described above. It is a good illustration of how to phrase a project dealing with a controversial issue — public interest litigation — in terms that are understandable and acceptable to funders.

BUDGET FOR A SHORT BOOK

	BUDGET	
1. Salaries (part-time)		
Research: 4 mo. @ $2,200/mo.	$8,800	
Writing and editing: 3 mo. @ $2,600/mo.	$7,800	
Secretary: 3 mo. @ $1,900/mo.	$5,700	
Print production and supervision: 1 mo. @ $2,000/mo.	$2,000	
Graphic design and art work:	$2,000	
Promotion and distribution:	$2,500	
Staff benefits @ 8%:	<u>$1,950</u>	
		$30,750
2. Office		
Rent: 8 mo. @ $500/mo.	$4,000	
Office supplies:	$ 559	
Computer rental: 3 mo. @ $280/mo.	$ 840	
Photocopy:	$ 360	
Telephone:	<u>$ 200</u>	
		$ 5,959
3. Production		
Typesetting: 60 pages @ $30/page:	$1,800	
Printing: 500 copies of 60-page book:	$2,400	
Binding (perfect): 500 copies @ $1.50	<u>$ 750</u>	
		$ 4,950
4. Other		
Travel to Hamilton and Ottawa:	$ 560	
Contingency:	<u>$4,000</u>	
		<u>$ 4,560</u>
TOTAL BUDGET		<u>$46,219</u>

PUBLIC INTEREST ADVOCACY HANDBOOK

A PROPOSAL FROM THE
CANADIAN ENVIRONMENTAL LAW
RESEARCH FOUNDATION

I. Introduction and Rationale

A real estate developer sued a citizen's group for $500,000 for conspiracy to interfere with its business. The group had asked its municipal council to prevent the development of ravine lots along the Credit River. When the case came to trial four years later, the developer's lawyers abandoned the suit against the group. Had the case against the citizen's group been successful, their homes and life savings might have been at stake. Also, such a precedent would threaten freedom of speech of residents before their elected representatives.

Even though the case was dropped and costs were awarded to the citizens, for four years they lived under a cloud of uncertainty. The lawsuit effectively stifled their work as a group over that period. Rather than submitting briefs to various public agencies on matters of environmental concern, the group was forced to spend most of its time trying to raise funds for the legal costs of its defence.

A community legal clinic provided legal services to members of the public who would not likely have been covered by the Ontario Legal Aid Plan. The clinic suggested that the tenants pay their rent into a trust fund rather than pay their landlord, because he failed to keep the premises in good repair.

In court, the landlord was successful on an application to evict the tenants. The court also ruled that the trust fund for rent was not authorized by the Ontario Landlord and Tenant Act. The landlord's lawyer asked the judge to award costs against the tenant's lawyer who was one of the staff of the legal clinic. Only after considerable discussion did the judge refuse to order the lawyer to personally pay the court costs. He admitted that the clinic was trying to fill a social need, but felt that it was irresponsible for an organization to undertake and sponsor litigation without having due regard to legal costs.

Environmental groups, civil rights organizations, consumer groups — all public interest groups and their lawyers — face unique legal problems seldom encountered by the average litigant (party to a lawsuit) or his or her lawyer. Many of the lawyers practising in community legal clinics or specializing in public interest law are young and inexperienced. It is often difficult for these lawyers to advise their clients about the unique problems that might arise, or to protect their clients and themselves from sophisticated forms of harassment designed to intimidate them. Very little has been written on the subject of some of these forms of harassment. They have not presented a serious problem until recently, when the frequency and consequences of public interest litigation have become more serious.

The staff of the Canadian Environmental Law Association and the Canadian Environmental Law Research Foundation have had nine years of experience in the practice of public interest law and have been called upon frequently to deal with questions such as, What can we say to the press while our case is in progress? What is my liability if I lose my case? Can I legally join a demonstration or picket line? Is it ethical to deliberately set up a test case situation?

II. Project description

We propose to write and publish a booklet explaining to both potential public interest litigants and their lawyers some of the issues that might arise during the course of public interest litigation, and what they can do to protect themselves.

The booklet will include chapters on the following subjects:

1. The Test Case: Is it legal? When the law is ambiguous or unclear, some segments of society take advantage of this to engage in practices which are oppressive. In such circumstances, the test case, taken not only to protect the rights of the individual acting as plaintiff, but to clarify the law for others in the same position, may be a useful step toward ending the oppressive practice.

Perhaps the best-known example in Canada was a case taken by the Canadian Civil Liberties Association on behalf of a black person who was refused service in an Ontario restaurant in the 1950s. However, engaging in this form of litigation may impose practical problems on the litigant and ethical problems for his or her legal advisors, particularly if they deliberately set up the factual situation to be used in court.

2. Picket Line Etiquette: What can I (or can't I) do during a demonstration? Rights to freedom of speech and freedom of assembly guarantee the right to peaceful and legal demonstrations. Public interest groups sometimes feel that such a peaceful demonstration is the best way, and in some cases the only way, to "get their message across." However, if such groups trespass or impede the flow of traffic they may be breaking the law.

Protestors and demonstrators have been arrested, sometimes properly and sometimes improperly. They should be aware of their rights and duties before undertaking this activity. Two lawyers have been charged with criminal and quasi-criminal offences in recent years as a result of their attendance at demonstrations to advise their clients. Both were acquitted, but only after costly legal proceedings.

3. Contempt: What can I (or can't I) say to the press about my case? Contempt is any act that is calculated to embarrass, hinder, or obstruct the court in the administration of justice, or which is calculated to lessen its authority or dignity. In public interest cases, clients are often approached by the press for comment while the case is in progress. They ask their lawyer for advice. Some guidelines as to the line between freedom of speech and contempt are given.

4. Defamation: Defamation is the offence of injuring a person's character or reputation by false and malicious statements. This includes libel, which is a written defamatory statement, and slander, which is a spoken statement. Public interest groups and their lawyers find more and more reasons to believe they may be sued for libel for anything they say, in an attempt to muzzle them on important issues.

5. Costs: What is the liability of the public interest litigant and his or her counsel for costs in a public interest lawsuit?

The general rule in Canada is that costs follow the event: that is, the loser in a civil action case pays approximately two-thirds of the legal expenses of the winner. The court in its discretion may make an exception in a public interest case.

On the other hand, some parties who have succeeded against public interest litigants have argued that the lawyer for the public interest group should personally bear the costs. Both the lawyer and client should know in advance the general rules regarding costs and special considerations that have been applied to public interest cases.

6. Charitable Status and Public Interest Activity: There are approximately 70,000 registered charitable non-profit organizations in Canada. In recent years, many of them have been tempted to engage in litigation or political activity as methods of furthering their goals. In some cases, involvement in public interest litigation or political activity could lead to revocation of a group's charitable status.

Community legal clinics and public interest lawyers are being asked for legal opinions on what effect certain activities might have on the group's charitable status. Moreover, many public interest lawyers in Canada practise as employees of charitable organizations and must advise their board of directors of the implications of certain activities.

III. Project budget*

Lawyer: 250 hours at $80 per hour	$20,000
Paralegal researcher: 130 hours at $40 per hour	$ 5,200
Secretary: 8 weeks at $460 per week	$ 3,680

Expenses:

(i) photocopying; 750 pp at $0.20 per page	$ 150
(ii) travel; 2 trips to Ottawa	$ 1,000
(iii) mileage; 300 miles at $0.40 per mile	$ 120
(iv) supplies and miscellaneous	$ 225
(v) long distance phone calls	$ 275

Publication: 50-page handbook, paperback size, 2-color cover, saddle-stitched (includes artwork, typesetting, page assembly, paper, printing, binding and cover), 2,000 copies	$ 3,685
Administration and Project Supervision: quotations, editing and proofreading, indexing, and all production duties	$ 2,100
Promotion: design and printing of flyer, media coverage	$ 1,500
TOTAL	**$37,935**

* **Note:** The budget format shown in Sample #3 should be used. A breakdown of the publication costs and written estimates from printers would also be included.

IV. Project schedule

1. Legal and paralegal research	6 weeks
2. First draft of manuscript	12 weeks
3. Editing of manuscript	4 weeks
4. Book design	2 weeks
5. Typesetting	6 weeks
6. Layout and art work	3 weeks
7. Printing	4 weeks
Total from starting date to completion:	**9 months**

V. The audience

With the assistance of colleagues at other public interest groups, we will establish a target list of individuals and public interest groups.

This would include Community Legal Clinics, the Consumers' Association of Canada, the Canadian Civil Liberties Association, the Ontario Federation of Labour, ratepayers, landlord and tenant groups, public interest lawyers, lawyers in private practice, law schools, and libraries. They will then be notified of the publication by mail, with telephone follow-up.

VI. Project staff

John Swaigen was one of the first lawyers in Canada to specialize in environmental law. He has practised for the past 15 years as general counsel to the Canadian Environmental Law Association and as a prosecutor and policy advisor for the Ontario Ministry of the Environment. In these roles, he has had first-hand experience conducting legal proceedings involving citizens' groups and lawful advocacy.

John Swaigen has been a consultant on environmental issues to the Economic Council of Canada, the Law Reform

Commission of Canada, the Public Interest Advocacy Centre, and environmental groups in Indonesia.

He is the author of several books and hundreds of papers, studies, and scholarly and popular articles on environmental, energy, and resource issues. While in university, he obtained training and experience in journalism as a reporter for the University of Toronto student newspaper. He has written a column for *Alternatives* magazine, and has contributed feature articles to the *Globe and Mail*, the *Toronto Star*, and the *Hamilton Spectator*.

VII. Anticipated results

With the help of this handbook, public interest groups and their lawyers will be better able to use public interest litigation to further their goals. Groups will also be less likely to succumb to those who would use the law for intimidation or harassment. Finally, this book will provide a small but significant contribution to the effectiveness of public interest groups in shaping public policy and making democracy work.

4

TYPES OF FUNDING

The type of funding you are looking for affects your funding strategy.

a. CORE FUNDING VERSUS PROJECT FUNDING

Core funding is the money that you need to operate an office and pay for rent, office supplies, computers, telephones, a secretary, and other day-to-day expenses. Projects, on the other hand, have a definite start and finish and involve a tangible end product. Things like speaking tours, writing and publishing a booklet, making a slide show or film, or undertaking specific research can be considered as projects.

Core funding is more difficult to obtain because the people who fund your daily operations have fewer ways to judge what you accomplished. Project funding is more popular because sponsors feel that they are playing a measurable role in a tangible activity, without getting locked into funding an ongoing activity which is difficult to evaluate.

Corporations, foundations, and the government all prefer to supply project funding because of the following reasons:

(a) Projects are finite. They may run for months or years but they don't go on indefinitely.

(b) Projects usually involve a tangible result which can be evaluated.

81

(c) Projects can be assigned a definite, adequate budget figure. Core costs tend to keep growing due to increases in staff, higher rent, and inflation.

However, government sources are generally more willing to fund core costs than either foundations or corporations.

Try to raise core funding from individual supporters or your membership, who might be more willing to provide this type of funding. You might have a money-making aspect to your group such as the sale of a publication or a nominal charge for certain services, which can go toward core costs. Any unallocated funds that you raise should be put toward your core costs or other activities that you can't fund directly.

If you are a service group, it is even harder for sponsors to evaluate whether their contributions were well spent. Provide them with statistics about how many people used your service, and provide client evaluations of your service. The best way for a service group to get around the difficulty of raising core funding is by describing part of the service as a project. The work of most staff people can be packaged as a project. A portion of your overhead or core costs is required to support the project staff person, and this portion of overhead becomes a legitimate project cost.

Many groups are burdened by a large portion of their budget labeled "administration, overhead, and core costs" which the donors find unappealing. Most of these should in full honesty be considered part of the project costs. For example, a group raising funds to print a booklet may wrongly assume that the only project cost is the printer's bill. In fact, it should include staff time to plan the project, research the facts, write the material, proofread changes, distribute the booklet, answer the phone and take requests for the booklet, write letters to people who comment on the booklet, and so on. It should also include a fair share of the rent, electrical, heat, and telephone bills, as well as postage and couriers. It should include the cost of an advertising and publicity campaign so that people know the booklets are available. Don't forget the computer, printer, desks, and chairs as well as office insurance and bookkeeping.

Think like a restaurateur. The cost of pizza includes far more than flour, cheese, tomato sauce, pepperoni, and mushrooms. It also includes the cook's labor, the waiter, the dishwasher, and the manager. It includes heat for the ovens and the restaurant. It includes advertising, a van for delivery, a phone, and much more. The pizza itself is only a fraction of the cost — often less than one-third of the total.

If you are a small group — with less than ten staff people — here is a simple way to budget your projects. Calculate your total annual overhead cost for office rent, heat, cleaning, insurance, telephone, postage, photocopying, etc. Add to that the salaries of secretaries, the bookkeeper, and the fundraiser. Divide this total by the number of "project staff" people. That will give you the overhead per project staff and make it easy to check whether you have budgeted project overhead correctly.

If all of that seems a bit elaborate, just remember that a lot of fundraising is really marketing. A cleverly packaged project will be easier to sell.

b. CAPITAL PROJECTS

Raising money for a building, filmmaking equipment, a computer system, a library, or some other expensive "thing" requires capital funding. In the fundraising trade, capital projects are referred to as "bricks and mortar" because, traditionally, they have been for buildings.

Large corporations and foundations used to participate heavily in capital campaigns because there was a definable need, a highly visible end product, and usually a brass plaque on the building recognizing the company's contribution. Capital projects are no longer popular because the sponsor's participation in them is expensive. Capital campaigns usually start at $500,000, and participation is going to cost a sponsor at least

$5,000. Many sponsors aren't willing or able to give that large a chunk of money, especially to a smaller, innovative group.

Many groups considering a capital campaign worry that it might bankrupt the organization's core or project funding. That's a legitimate concern because, if it isn't properly managed, it may do just that. However, a well-managed capital campaign can be used to attract new funders and approach sources that specialize in capital funding. If it's done right, it should increase your group's public profile and broaden your funding base.

The next few pages will give you some tips and warnings about capital campaigns, but they are by no means a road map. Capital fundraising is specialized and sophisticated and you should look beyond the information presented here before making the decision to take on a capital project.

The first thing to remember is that you are competing with large, established institutions such as universities, hospitals, and YM-YWCAs.

The second thing to remember is that you can't build half a building or use half a piece of equipment — a capital campaign is an all or nothing proposition. If you buy a building, for example, but can't afford heat, electricity, or staff, the building is useless. Your funding proposal must indicate your plans for operation and maintenance of the project after it is built or bought.

Indicate in your proposal that you have set up a trust fund and name the bank and branch. You can invest this money and collect interest until you have reached your objective. Set a target date that gives you enough time to have a good go at it, and if you don't raise all the money by that time, or at least 75% of the total, *give back* the money you have raised, with a note of thanks. That's how it works.

REMEMBER, DONATIONS FOR A CAPITAL CAMPAIGN CANNOT BE USED FOR ANY OTHER PURPOSE.

Tell your sponsors how their contribution will be recognized and try to think up appropriate and inexpensive ways to do this. For instance, if you are building a library, you might hand out bookmarks for the first year listing your sponsors. Sponsors of a capital campaign do deserve a little extra recognition!

You can't build half a building.

Matching funding schemes are often used for capital campaigns. If you need to raise $100,000 for building renovations, consider the following pyramid scheme:

3 sponsors	@	$10,000	=	$ 30,000
6 sponsors	@	$ 5,000	=	$ 30,000
12 sponsors	@	$ 2,500	=	$ 30,000
General contributions			=	$ 10,000
TOTAL =				$100,000

Then you would carefully select at least three potential sponsors to approach for $10,000 and so on. One advantage of a matching scheme is peer pressure. Corporations and wealthy individuals have their pride. Before you can put together a matching funding scheme that will work, you have to know the money-giving scene well. You have to know which donors are leaders in innovative funding and who will follow their example.

You might also break up your funding objective by source, indicating, for example, that you expect to raise 30% from corporations, 30% from foundations, 30% from individuals, and 10% from government contributions.

If your group has undertaken any sort of capital campaign previously, give a brief history of this success in your funding proposal. That will tell potential sponsors that you have the experience and the capability to carry out what you are proposing.

If your organization has never conducted a capital campaign before, do a little "market research" first. Select a number of foundations and corporations that you think you might approach. Write to them and say your group is considering undertaking a capital campaign to build such and such; ask if they have a capital funding program and if they might consider an appeal from your group. You want to find out what kind of money is available for what you are proposing to do. They will respect your initiative.

If they indicate that they do contribute to capital programs, try to find out what size contribution they have made in the past, and to whom. It is generally easier to get this kind of information from foundations than corporations. Corporations do have policies on this, but they don't make their policies public as some foundations do.

Phone the person who answered your letter and politely ask a few exploratory questions. Try to get a feeling for whether the foundation is interested in your capital project, and try to find out what they have done in the past. You've got nothing to lose by asking a few polite questions — and before you launch a capital campaign, you've got a lot to learn.

Alternatively, you could hire a fundraising consultant to do a feasibility study on the capital campaign you are considering. The consultant will make sure you have thought through all the important aspects, and then will interview leaders in the philanthropic community to see if they would support the project.

Capital campaigns should not begin on impulse. Once you launch a capital campaign you are putting your group's reputation to a test in the philanthropic community. It's hard to say just what the repercussions of failure would be, but you don't want to fail, so investigate first.

There are fundraising consulting firms that specialize in capital campaigns and this is one area in which experienced fundraising consultants are well worth their fee. If nobody in your organization is experienced in capital fundraising, it is probably advisable to at least have an exploratory meeting with a consultant. Tips for working with consultants are given in chapter 11.

In a capital campaign, the first donation is the hardest to get. One corporation, foundation, or government agency has to stick its neck out and endorse your project by making that first donation. Nobody wants to make the first move. Try to get that first donation, or at least a commitment on paper, before you launch your campaign fully and publicly.

c. DEFICIT FUNDING

Some people can live comfortably with debt, be it personal debt or organizational debt, but it is very bad for a non-profit group to be in debt. As a registered charitable organization, you don't have the right to make a profit and you don't have the right to live in debt either. However, if you are reading this, you probably have a debt, so what do you do about it?

First of all, don't let it get any bigger. Don't let it grow because it can get out of hand. Second, look for ways to cut expenses in your operation: reduce salaries or staff for a period of time, cut back on long distance calls or travel, make do with that old piece of equipment for a while longer. Put the money saved toward the debt.

Now try to raise money to cover the debt. You can't get corporations or foundations to make a direct contribution toward your deficit. They simply won't do it because they are afraid they will be putting money down a bottomless hole. Most foundations state explicitly in their guidelines that they will not fund deficits. Any funding agency that asks for a financial statement wants to make sure you don't have a deficit.

Deficit contributions — putting money down a bottomless hole.

88

You *can* ask individuals to contribute. If you have a paying membership, three to six months after your normal membership campaign you might do a special campaign for funds to pay back your debt. It's a bit embarrassing, but with a lot of tact you can succeed. Indicate the total you need to raise to cover your debt and how much each person needs to contribute to put you "in the black" again.

It's important that the tone be appropriate for your membership, and that you discuss the deficit in a businesslike manner. The tone should be: "We have a problem. This is how we're going to solve it. This is what we need from you to help us solve it." It is essential that you be firm and confident in your approach to your members. Don't cry on their shoulders, because they've already done their bit.

Sample #5 is an example of a letter to members asking for contributions to a debt.

You can also try to pay back your deficit by allocating a portion of it to each project. If you have a 2% deficit, write into your project budget "contribution to deficit" and make that figure 2% of the total project cost. In this way you are being honest about it. Some people try to pay back a debt by padding budgets. That practice is dishonest and unethical and it offends donors.

Running an organization with a debt is depressing and demoralizing. DON'T IGNORE IT BECAUSE IT WON'T GO AWAY. Confront the problem. Figure out a way to get out of it, and see your plan through.

Once a group projected a deficit in an attempt to pressure potential donors to contribute. The line was: "If you don't give now we are going to go under," and it wasn't really true. To make matters worse, this tactic was being used in an approach to a bank! There is no real temptation to try such a tactic: it doesn't even work. Don't cry wolf!

SAMPLE #5
LETTER TO RAISE DEFICIT FUNDS

Society to Save Dead Elm Trees
1 Elmsvale Crescent
Elmada, MI 04309

Dear Mr. Snow,

We are pleased to report that we now have a continuing membership of 500 individuals and have succeeded in securing 94 new members for our organization.

As an active member, you are committed to preserving the natural heritage of the rural Ontario landscape by helping to preserve dead elm trees. It costs $100 to purchase a dead elm tree and prevent its ruin. Last year, The Society to Save Dead Elm Trees purchased 90 dead elm trees. Their locations, should you wish to visit or photograph them, are indicated in the enclosed brochure.

It appears that we were a little over-enthusiastic in our purchases last year. Our Dead Elm Tree Purchase Fund fell $1,000 short of its goal of $9,000. We are currently operating with a deficit of $1,000 and are making a special appeal for money to cover this deficit.

As you know, dead elm trees provide food and shelter for woodpeckers, scenic perches for hawks, and much-needed homes for wayward raccoons. We are asking you, as a loyal member, at this time, to contribute an additional $25 to the Dead Elm Tree Purchase Fund. Of the ten trees which are not yet paid for, three are particularly significant as they are located along Highway 401 and are viewed and enjoyed by thousands of people every day.

We would be very grateful if you could give us a little extra support at this time. Thank you for your continuing interest in our society.

Sincerely,

Jane Woods

Jane Woods

d. SOLE SOURCE FUNDING

Some Canadian organizations have the mixed blessing of receiving all of their money, or most of it, from one source. This occurs most often with government funding agencies, although some foundations and individuals will provide substantial support to one group for a few years.

We are all familiar with government funding programs, which often provide the seed money for new, innovative groups. Unfortunately, many of these groups come and go because they don't plan their financial future and don't try to broaden their financial support base until their grant has almost run out. Groups that have been solely funded by one government agency for a few years are often unwilling to face up to reality when they are informed that they will be on their own. Often, much time is wasted in fruitless lobbying — time that would be better spent developing and implementing a new funding strategy.

Occasionally, a wealthy individual or member of a board of directors will provide the bulk of the funding for a group. You may think, "We should be so lucky!" But the fact is that this person can end up having far too much control over the policies and direction of the group because he or she controls the purse strings.

In the United States, tax laws prevent this situation by stipulating that a public charity cannot get more than one-third of its funding from one source. Contact your local IRS office and ask for Publication 557 to get the details. The rules change, so it's worth checking.

If you depend on sole source funding, take a careful look at the situation, weigh the pros and cons, and consider developing a broader base. You need to be sure that your funding source does not have a controlling role in determining your direction and does not restrict your ability to carry out your mandate. Before that source of money dries up, you had better be prepared if you are to survive.

5

DEVELOPING A
FUNDRAISING STRATEGY

a. STRATEGY IS THE KEY TO SUCCESS

A large number of organizations still function without a strategy of any sort — either a strategic plan for the whole organization, or simply a fundraising strategy. A strategy is critical to the organization's effectiveness; operating without one is like going on a trip without a road map.

Joyce recently worked with a social service agency to help them develop a fundraising strategy. Working with a fundraising committee of the board, she assessed the organization's needs, strengths, and weaknesses and tried to match that to funding sources and fundraising techniques.

The consultation had a dramatic outcome. It was as though the fundraising strategy development process had held a mirror up to the organization and gave it a full and accurate picture of itself. In the previous year it had undergone some major changes, including —

- Hiring its first full-time staff
- Merging with another organization
- Increasing its annual budget by 700%

In one year, the organization was proposing to —

- Host a national conference for the first time
- Double its annual budget
- Begin fundraising outside the government sectors

- Move from 100% government funding to 100% funding from other sources in one year

When that picture was presented to the board members, they understood why they were feeling exhausted and overwhelmed. They were quick to lead the discussion about what they could give up or put on the back burner. They realized they couldn't do all that in one year with limited resources.

The first step in developing a strategy is to answer honestly the following questions:

(a) Where have we been?

(b) Where are we going?

(c) What do we have to work with?

(d) What's going on outside the organization that's going to affect us?

(e) What is our best course of action?

A strategy can be developed at the program or project level for a function such as fundraising, or on an organization-wide basis. Just keep in mind, it needs to be done. You will never feel like you "have time" for working out a strategy. It will always seem like an abstract, academic exercise. So why bother? Because it is one of the smartest things you can do for your organization. It will give you a way of thinking about your organization that will enhance your ability to survive and it is an essential tool for organizations committed to quality and effectiveness.

b. FUNDRAISING STRATEGY MATRIX

Your fundraising strategy will be the outcome of an analysis of factors inside and outside your organization that determine what you are going to sell and to whom you are going to sell it. By taking into account the strengths and weaknesses of your organization and recognizing the external factors which will influence your fundraising success, a fundraising strategy will tell you how to get the best return on your fundraising effort.

The fundraising strategy matrix is a tool to help you identify and evaluate your fundraising sources and methods as listed below.

1. Fundraising choices

(a) Source: individuals

    (i) Direct mail

    (ii) Special events

    (iii) Product sales

    (iv) Bequests, insurance, and other planned giving

    (v) Canvass

    (vi) Major donors or special names (large gifts)

    (vii) Telephone campaigns

    (viii) Paid advertising

    (ix) Free Public Service Announcements (PSAs) in newspapers, magazines, radio, TV

    (x) Telethons and other broadcast direct response

    (xi) In Memoriam and celebration cards and commemorations

    (xii) Fee for service work

    (xiii) Bingo, raffles, casinos, and other gambling

(b) Source: corporations

    (i) Project proposals

    (ii) Matching employee contributions

    (iii) Joint promotions

    (iv) Sponsorship of events or publications

(v) Fee for service work

(vi) In-kind goods and services

(c) Source: foundations and governments

(i) Project proposals

(d) Source: Other organizational donors

(i) Service clubs

(ii) United Way (as regular funders or for special grants)

(iii) Religious groups

(iv) Unions

(v) Employee charitable funds

(vi) Professional groups (such as Business Women's Association)

(vii) Seniors' and Retirees' Associations

(viii) Other non-profits

(e) Source: Productive Enterprise or Community Economic Development

(i) Consulting work

(ii) Manufacturing or products

(iii) Sales, shops, vending machines

(iv) Services

(v) Other quasi-business income sources

2. Evaluation

You can evaluate each source/method's potential for your organization by considering it in relation to the following factors. Some of the factors won't apply to certain source/methods.

(a) Contacts

Are there staff or board members in the funding organization with whom your people have an established relationship?

(b) Market

What is the correlation between the people you serve and the people the funder serves?

(c) Profile

What is your visibility within your community of interest? Will the name of your organization, your staff, your president, your programs be recognized by members of key constituencies? Are you in the media?

(d) Information

Do you have the basic information on this funding source — annual report, brochures, application forms, press clippings, names of donations officers? The information should be no more than two years old.

(e) Criteria

How well do you fit the funder's criteria? Which criteria don't you fit? How important are these criteria?

(f) Skill

Do your staff and volunteers have the requisite skills for this type of fundraising — proposal writing, corporate and foundation research, meeting skills, presentation skills. Do staff and volunteers have enough time? Do they need training? Are there tasks they would never be comfortable doing? Do you need to recruit new people with skills or contacts?

(g) Areas of interest

How well do your areas of interest fit the funder's areas of interest? This question is more general than the one concerning criteria. If the funder's areas of interest are not defined, try to establish this by analyzing the pattern of their donations over the past few years.

(h) Policy

Do any of your organization's stated policies, positions, or beliefs conflict with the funder's stated policies, positions, or beliefs? Review speeches, bulletins, press clippings, and any other available information. This element is critical for your advocacy activities. Do your positions conflict with the stance of the current government?

(i) History

What is the fundraising history of your organization? What fundraising techniques and what funding sources and methods have been successful in the past?

(j) Means

Do the prospective donors have the kind of money you are looking for? Is the money out there for what you are trying to do?

(k) Projects and programs

Do you have your activities packaged into fundable projects and programs? Which of your programs and projects will be most attractive to funders?

(l) Competition

What other organizations are competing for the same charitable dollar? Can you hold your own with them?

(m) Lists

Do you have good, up-to-date lists of members and potential members? Do you have contacts in other organizations who would "swap" mailing lists with you?

(n) Geography

Does your location give you direct access to many of your funders? Does it make your group a priority for any government or foundation funds?

(o) Budget and resources

Do you have the money to invest in this form of fundraising? Can you wait while a long-term process slowly ripens or do you need an immediate cash boost?

(p) Donor recognition

What are appropriate, ethical methods that your group can use to give the donor extra publicity, well-deserved ego satisfaction, or a commemorative honor for a loved one?

(q) Responsibilities and administration in multi-level organizations

If your group has local, regional, national, international, or other levels, how do you avoid turf wars? Will a donor activity be done more effectively at this or another level, balancing local contacts and economies of scale? Will the donor be confused by multiple donation requests from different parts of the organization?

(r) Donor records

Do you have access to information on appeals to this or similar donors? If you get a sudden influx of new donors, will you be able to keep up with the work of entering information, sending thank-you letters, and making repeat contacts on time?

The fundraising strategy matrix can be used in a worksheet format to evaluate fundraising source/methods in relation to *your* organization and in relation to each other (see Sample #6). You can add to, reduce, or change the evaluation factors to suit your particular circumstances.

Work through the strategy matrix with a group such as a fundraising committee. List the evaluation factors down the left-hand side. Then choose the source/methods you want to evaluate and list them across the top. Work your way down the list of evaluation factors, discussing each one as it concerns the different source/methods and then deciding whether it is a plus (+) or a minus (-). When you have considered all the factors for each source/method, tally the pluses and minuses, then list in order the source/methods that got the most plus signs. Apply your judgment and decide which sources/methods to pursue.

Developing a fundraising strategy requires judgment. There is no linear formula that will give you the "right" answer. The strategy matrix is simply a tool to help you think it through logically and make a more informed choice.

c. FUNDRAISING STRATEGY THINK TANK

Another way to develop a strategy is through a think tank. Bring together people from outside your organization who are knowledgeable about your issues, your constituencies, and fundraising. Ask them to commit just one evening to help your group come up with a fundraising strategy.

Samples #7 and #8 are from a think tank held by the Legal Education and Action Fund (LEAF). Sample #7 is the agenda followed by LEAF. Each small work group dealt with a different source/method. To guide their discussion, each small group had a list of specific questions. When the whole workshop regrouped after discussion, there was a great deal of excitement and positive energy in the room. Many innovative and creative ideas emerged. From the reports of the small groups, a collective road map gradually emerged with clearly marked barriers and passages.

To close the session, we distributed the thank-you card shown in Sample #8. Inside was a short questionnaire by which people could offer to provide time, money, or contacts, or simply say they had a fun evening. These were collected at the door.

SAMPLE #6
FUNDRAISING STRATEGY MATRIX

	INDIVIDUALS			CORPORATIONS		GOVERNMENT
	Direct mail	Special events	Canvass	Project proposal	Matching employee contributions	Project proposal
Contacts	n/a	+	n/a	-	-	+
Market	+	+	+	-	-	-
Profile	-	-	-	-	-	-
Information	+	n/a	-	+	+	+
Criteria	n/a	n/a	n/a	+	+	-
Skill	+	+	+	+	+	+
Areas of interest	+	-	-	-	-	-
Policy	+	+	+	+	+	+
History	-	+	+	+	n/a	+
Means	+	+	+	+	-	+
Projects and programs	-	-	-	-	-	-
Competition	-	+	-	-	+	-
Lists	+	n/a	n/a	n/a	n/a	n/a
Geography	n/a	+	+	n/a	n/a	-
Budget & resources	-	-	+	+	+	+
Donor recognition	n/a	+	n/a	+	+	+
Multi-level	-	+	+	-	-	-
Donor records	+	+	+	+	+	+

SAMPLE #7
AGENDA FOR FUNDRAISING
STRATEGY WORKSHOP

AGENDA
LEAF FUNDRAISING STRATEGY WORKSHOP

TIME	ACTIVITY	STAFF
5:00-5:20	Reception	Everyone
5:20-5:30	Assembly Introduction of guests Purpose of meeting	Marilou McPhedran
5:30-5:40	Our vision of LEAF	Nancy Jackman
5:40-5:50	Achievements to date Current situation	Shelagh Day
5:50-6:00	Task description Division to small work groups	Joyce Young
6:00-7:40	Work in small groups	Facilitators Recorders
7:40-8:00	Plans for follow-up Reports from work groups Cards for guest follow-up Thank-you and closing	Marilou McPhedran Facilitators

SAMPLE #8
THANK-YOU CARD

Please complete this card and leave it with a LEAF representative before you go. Thank you so much for your guidance and suggestions this evening.

Yes, I am prepared to serve on the fundraising task force ❑

Yes, I am prepared to serve on a special events committee ❑

Yes, you can call me for advice and ideas ❑

Try me; I can help LEAF with_____

Name_____

Telephone number_____

By the end of the evening, LEAF had some money, a rough fundraising strategy, and a new, high-powered fundraising committee that was ready to roll. Not bad for a night's work!

d. CORPORATE FUNDRAISING STRATEGY

Corporate donations are an important source of income for non-profit organizations. Don't overestimate their value, however. In the United States, only 4.7% of all the private sector donations come from corporations. That constitutes over $6 billion out of $129.88 billion total. More than 80% of the money comes from individuals. Foundations give 7.6%. Bequests total 6.8%. The proportions are very similar in Canada.

1. Brainstorming

The first part of your corporate fundraising strategy must be determining which corporations are most likely to consider funding your group. One good way to approach this question is through a technique called brainstorming. It's best to conduct this process with a group of people, perhaps your whole staff or board of directors as well as a few outsiders who have a broader view of the organization. Let your imagination run free and get everybody to say anything that comes into their minds. Record everything on a flip chart. The technique will produce some ridiculous and some clever results.

Begin with your statement of objectives. If your objectives are clear and specific, they will help you and your fellow brainstormers to consider the question: "Who does the organization serve?" For example:

- If you run a daycare center, you serve children and parents.
- If you run a rape crisis center, you serve the victims of rape and the community at large.
- If you run a gallery or theater, you serve your patrons and the community at large.

102

- If you run the Society to Save Dead Elm Trees, you serve the people who love the dead elm trees (as well as the wayward raccoons).

Whenever possible, those who benefit directly from your group should pay at least a portion of your annual budget. This funding, however, is rarely enough. Otherwise, you could become a profit-making business! You need to find other sources. So, the next question you toss to your brainstorming group is: "Who has a vested interest in the people we are serving?"

- If you run a daycare center, manufacturers and retailers of children's toys, books, clothes, diapers, baby powder, and so on have a vested interest in children and parents. So do the companies whose employees would not be able to work if they had no daycare.

- If you run a rape crisis center, manufacturers and retailers of women's clothes, jewelry, and cosmetics, and publishers of women's books and magazines all have a specific, vested interest in women.

- If you run a gallery, manufacturers of canvas, artists' supplies, picture frames, and paper have an interest.

- If you run the Society to Save Dead Elm Trees, tourist industries have an interest.

In this way you will get a list of business and industry sectors which should be interested in your work since your clients form their market.

Not all corporations are equally interested in giving. Many give little or nothing.

In the United States, the pharmaceutical industry is the most generous. It gives 10.5% of all the corporate donations in the country. That amounts to about $207 million out of the total $1.975 billion that corporations give charities in the United States. Here is a list from the Conference Board's 1994 survey of 1993 donations, based on total dollars given:

- Pharmaceuticals   10.5%
- Petroleum/Gas/Mining   8.9
- Telecommunications   8.4
- Food/Beverage/Tobacco   7.6
- Computers/Office Equipment   7.3
- Chemicals   7.1
- Transportation   7.0
- Electrical Machinery   6.6
- Insurance   6.1
- Finance   4.8
- Retail/Wholesale   4.8
- Banking   4.4
- Utilities   3.5
- Paper Products   2.9
- Primary Metals   2.6
- Printing/Publishing/Media   2.4
- Other Manufacturing   2.3
- Nonelectrical Machinery   1.2
- Other Services   0.8
- Transportation   0.7

In Canada, the banking industry gives almost 30% of all corporate donations. That is almost $36 million out of $123.8 million total donations in 1992. All together, 70% of all Canadian corporate donations come from only seven industries, according to The Canadian Centre for Business and the Community.

The biggest corporate givers in Canada (based on a percentage of total dollars given) are the following:

- Banking   28.9%
- Petroleum products   11.3
- Beverage and tobacco   8.3
- Communication   7.1
- Insurance   5.1
- Primary metals   4.7
- Transportation   4.5

This generosity is measured in total dollars given. As a percentage of their pre-tax profits, Canadian banks only rate tenth. The biggest proportional givers include:

- Credit unions   3.12%
- Food   2.95
- Computers/office equipment   1.48
- Trust companies   1.45
- Mining   1.33
- Real estate/investment   1.15
- Beverage and tobacco   1.12
- Oil and gas   1.11
- Machinery, transport, auto manufacturing   1.05
- Banking   0.93

Over 400 Canadian businesses have declared themselves "Caring Companies" as part of the IMAGINE campaign. These corporations have agreed to give charities donations which total 1% of their pre-tax profits (averaged over three years). Most companies give much less. As a result, these 400 companies give 40% of all corporate gifts. For a list of these companies, contact the Canadian Centre for Philanthropy (see the Appendix for the address and phone number).

Please do not send a form letter to all these companies. One corporate donor estimates that they get 10,000 applications a year. That works out to one every ten minutes. This is far too much for the donors to handle. Many of the corporate donors are very frustrated at the amount of time they waste dealing with requests that should never have come to the company in the first place.

Canadian Pacific Charitable Foundation receives one thousand applications each year and "many are very poor quality," according to Hollie L. Zuorro, donations officer. "They don't state their name, address, charitable number, purpose, goals and objectives, accomplishments, or reason for fundraising. They do not define their clients or service area. And, they do not explain their local, regional, or national affiliations."

To get funding, get a realistic view of the community needs and discuss this openly in your request. Form alliances and partnerships with like groups. Trim down your list to the most likely donors before you send applications. Here's how.

2. Paring the list

With your list of interested businesses in hand, your next question should be: "Of those businesses, which ones are in a good financial position?" After all, a corporation that is losing money isn't likely to give you any. This is where the research begins. If you have a fundraising committee made up of business people, they will know who's making money in the different sectors. Your local Chamber of Commerce is a very good source of information. In Canada, you can also look at corporate annual reports or in the Survey of Industrials.

The next question is: "Do we have a contact in that company?" Many granters automatically give high priority to an organization where someone they know is involved. Again, your fundraising committee may be able to name a person in that company or provide an introduction.

Look among your board, volunteers, friends, and (if it is appropriate) the people you serve. You might find people who work for the companies, buy their products in quantity, sell them supplies, or have a friend on the inside. While a high-ranking contact is the most influential, many companies give preference to charities supported by their employees at any level. Corporate employees can often get matching grants for non-profit organizations they support with time or money. For example, Lotus Development Canada triples its staff's donations. They'll give $2 for every $1 an employee gives.

Look for the companies with the largest number of employees in your area. Check your local municipal government's business development office. Phone and ask the person who answers to give you information without connecting you to the person. Ask for the name and title of the contact person for donations. Check the spelling carefully. Start building up a file.

Now your list is shorter but more focused. Phone and request a copy of each company's annual report if you don't have it. Sometimes major newspapers like the *Globe and Mail*, *Wall Street Journal*, or the *Financial Post* will run a corporate annual report coupon. If you send in this coupon you will automatically receive the annual reports of many companies.

Many of the larger consumer-oriented corporations have quite specific areas of interest and limit their giving to these areas. Others define several areas and allocate a predetermined percentage of their donations budget to each of those areas. Not all companies will state their areas of interest, but, with a little research, you can find out where they stand. Read the list of sponsors in the annual reports of groups similar to yours and read the society columns in a major newspaper: both these sources can yield information on who is giving funds to whom.

If you have information on corporate areas of interest for charitable giving, put those companies that contribute to your field at the top of your list.

3. Joint promotions

A company may want to use your group's name in association with its product in exchange for donating a percentage of the proceeds to your group. This is called a joint promotion. The company believes that being associated with your group will give it an advantage in the marketplace. Of course, you have to decide whether *you* want to be associated with *them!* Consider your members' feelings on the subject and check it out before you proceed.

If you decide to go ahead, get a written contract laying out the details. Will you have any input on the ad campaign? How will the income to your group be calculated, and how often will it be paid? What period of time does the joint promotion cover? Even if you decide against joint promotions, you can expect most companies to want some promotional value for their contributions. Solid recognition of corporate contributions will give your group a competitive advantage in the fundraising market.

4. In-kind donations

Many companies are happy to donate their products, services, employee time, building space, and leftover supplies. Often these donations in-kind total far more than cash donations. Examples include printing, computers, software, fax machines, airline tickets, office space, manufacturing equipment, food, safety supplies, paint, and just about anything else you can imagine.

Make a list of what you need. Ask your current supporters, and other businesses in your community.

Three organizations can assist you. They arrange for charities to receive donations worth over $260 million. Contact them for more information:

John Page, Executive Director
In Kind Canada
7003 Cadiz Crescent
Mississauga, ON L5N 1Y3
Tel: (905) 567-9919
Fax: (905) 826-0272

Gifts in Kind America
700 North Fairfax Street
Alexandria, VA 22314
Tel: (703) 836-2121

Gary C. Smith, President
The National Association for the Exchange of
Industrial Resources (NAEIR)
560 McClure Street
Gailsburg, IL 61401
Tel: (309) 343-0704

5. Follow up on rejection

Corporations, foundations, and other organizational donors often turn down grant requests with a letter that says something like "Our funds are committed for this year." Too many groups interpret this as a permanent rejection.

They may be willing to give. Perhaps you applied too late. If you have received support from them in the past, they may have a policy that limits the number of years in a row in which they will donate to the same groups. Potential donors might welcome an application in future. Follow up any such letters with a note to ask if you should reapply, and, if so, at what time of year.

e. FOUNDATIONS

There is still quite a mystique about foundations: where they get their money and to whom they give it. Even the word "foundation" is confusing, because there are foundations that raise money and foundations that give it away. This section deals with the latter.

There are four types of foundations:

(a) those set up by a family

(b) those designed to serve a specific community or geographical area

(c) those set up by a corporation

(d) those established to foster a certain interest.

Foundations tend to specialize their funding in one or more of three ways:

(a) by restricting their giving to a geographical area

(b) by defining specific areas of interest

(c) by defining the type of funding they will give, i.e., capital costs or project costs.

Many foundations have a calendar fiscal year, and many only meet once a year to make decisions on funding requests, so the fall is a good time to approach them.

Canada has far fewer large foundations than the United States. Few Canadian foundations have staff, so a lot of your contact with Canadian foundations will be through correspondence.

The most comprehensive written source on Canadian foundations is the *Canadian Directory to Foundations*, published by The Canadian Centre for Philanthropy (see the Appendix for the publisher's address). The directory also includes a section on American Foundations and one on American Granting Agencies. It has a good bibliography of resource books on foundations around the world.

The Canadian Centre for Philanthropy also operates a resource center, offers training, and publishes books on fundraising and management for non-profit groups. Ask about their computer-assisted research on foundations. Canadian fundraisers can also find useful information in directories published by Rainforest Publications of Vancouver. This includes information on corporate donors, private foundations, and employee charitable trusts. Their toll-free number is 1-800-655-7729.

American groups should get *The Foundation Directory*, prepared by The Foundation Center (see the Appendix for the address). The Foundation Center's libraries keep sets of IRS records (Form 990PF) for all foundations in the United States. Located in New York and Washington, D.C., these libraries are open to the public and are free. Only about 900 of the 40,000 foundations in the United States publish annual reports, so the information returns are an important data source. The Foundation Center's field offices in Cleveland, Atlanta, and San Francisco keep foundation information returns for their regions.

As well, The Foundation Center operates a library net-work of over 200 cooperating collections in North America. All are open to the public and are free. To check on the location nearest you, in the United States you can call their toll-free number at 1-800-424-9836. From outside the United States call (212) 620-4230. You can also access the Foundation Center's World Wide Web Internet connection http://fdncenter.org. This includes *Philanthropy News Digest* which provides summaries of articles in the major media. The Center's databases are also available via DIALOG, an on-line service of Knight-Ridder Information, Inc.

Once you have the appropriate directory, decide which general categories best describe your group's work, such as health, education, welfare, or ecology, and go through the areas of interest index. Select the foundations that list your category as one of their areas of interest and write to them requesting their annual report and any other information on their funding programs. Many foundations do not publish annual reports or funding guidelines, but it is worth asking.

The amount of information foundations will volunteer varies widely. Some are very explicit about how much they gave, to whom, and for what. Others will be vague or not send anything. The foundations that do respond are your first best bet, and once you read their information you will have a better idea whether it's worthwhile to approach them.

Read the foundation's annual report carefully. Look at the type of groups and activities the foundation is funding and the dollar range of the grants. Look for any comments on the foundation's priorities for the future and note any titles it has given to a grants program, for instance, "Social Development and the Environment." You should use all these details to tailor your funding proposal to the programs of the particular foundation.

In Canada, you have access to further information. In-come tax legislation requires foundations to file information on their income, their assets, and their contributions. That information, or part of it, is public, so contact Revenue Canada and ask for the foundation's Public Information Return, Form T3010. The government employees you deal with may not be used to giving out this information — be firm and persistent.

A few foundations are very innovative and will fund things that nobody else will touch. Most foundations are conservative and tend to give most of their money to large, traditional campaigns such as university research, health organizations, and hospitals. Most are quite specific about whom they will fund. Other than that, it's impossible to generalize. There are some large foundations in Canada, and there are a few very large foundations in the United States that accept requests from Canadian groups. Finding the one that's going to give to you is a matter of doing your homework and getting lucky.

f. GOVERNMENT

Governments reflect current social issues of high priority in their funding programs more quickly and closely than either foundations or corporations. It usually takes much longer to get a response to an application for funds and much longer yet to actually get the promised money from government sources. Government sources also require much more detailed reports on activities and financial transactions. After all, you are spending the taxpayer's dollar. If you do fit their terms of reference, they tend to give out worthwhile sums of money.

Most government funding programs have brochures available indicating eligibility, criteria and guidelines, areas of interest and application procedures. Get that information before you decide whether to apply. Government funding programs often have field officers who do have time to see you, and they will help you figure out if you are eligible and under what program. They will help you with your application.

112

Make good use of these people and try to sell them on your project because they make the initial recommendation on your proposal.

If what your group is proposing to do fits in with a policy statement made by a high official or made in a government report, point this out in your application. Don't forget to ask your local political representative to endorse your project.

g. SERVICE CLUBS

Hundreds of organizations exist for a combination of community service and fellowship. No strategy would be complete without considering asking them for support. They may be able to give an outright cash grant. They may offer volunteer labor. They may create a special event to raise money for you or with you.

Most of them prefer to provide help at the local level, which makes them good resources for small town groups, or non-profit organizations working in specific neighborhoods. A few will give outside their home base, and some, like the Lions and Rotary, have substantial international development programs.

Most prefer to give to projects that will directly help people, especially children. The donations they give may be smaller than corporations or foundations, but occasionally they give hundreds of thousands of dollars.

Here is a partial list to get your mind running: the Ancient Arabic Order of the Nobles of the Mystic Shrine (more commonly known at the Shriners), fraternities and sororities like Beta Sigma Phi, the Blue Knights (police motorcycle riders), B'nai Brith, Civitan Club, Club Richelieu, car owners such as the Corvette Club, the Elks and their companion women's group the Royal Order of Purple, the Independent Order of Foresters (which runs a giant insurance company), the Independent Order of Odd Fellows, JayCees, Kinsmen Club, Kiwanis International, Knights of Columbus, Knights of

Pythias, the Lions Club International (the world's largest service organization), the Loyal Order of Moose, Masonic and Military Orders of Knights of the Red Cross of Constantine, Optimists, Quota Club, Rotary Club, the Royal Canadian Legion, University Women's Clubs, Variety Club, veterans' associations, Women's Institute, Ysmen (senior members of the YMCA), and Zonta International.

h. EMPLOYEE CHARITABLE FUNDS

Inside many corporations, groups of employees raise money to give to charity. They often support the United Way. In addition, many Employee Charitable Funds give large grants to a wide variety of other groups. This is the employee's own money, not the corporate giving budget.

For example, the Telephone Pioneers of America is the world's largest industry-related volunteer organization. Their membership (743,000 in the United States and 80,000 members in Canada) includes people who work for any phone company. Their motto: "Answering the Call of Those in Need."

Altogether, they raised nearly $9 million and volunteered more than 31 million hours toward providing quality services to the lonely, people with disabilities, and the disadvantaged.

As of 1994, the Pioneers had four key areas of focus: literacy, the environment, the hearing impaired, and drug and substance abuse. However, they take on many different projects.

There are hundreds of similar groups. Rainforest Publications publishes a Directory of Employee Charitable Trusts, listing 580 employee operated trusts in Canada. For details see the Appendix.

i. THE UNITED WAY

Even if your group does not get regular United Way funding, you may be able to get support from them. Depending on the city, they may provide special grants, volunteer training, or in-kind donations. They may be willing to serve as a match-maker and introduce you to leaders from corporations, unions, employee funds, or foundations.

All of this may be provided in a friendly manner with no strings attached. In some cases they will request that you not compete with them for the same donors at the same time of year.

In many communities, there are various alternatives to the United Way that are also worth approaching. These groups may be based on religious principles, such as the United Jewish Appeal, The Salvation Army Red Feather, Catholic Charities, Episcopal Charities, and so on. They may be based on ethnic or racial groups, such as the United Black Fund of America.

j. RELIGIOUS GROUPS

Many churches, convents, synagogues, mosques, and other religious groups give money, space in their buildings, and other kinds of support to other charities. They support social justice programs, food banks, arts groups, health care, AIDS, alcohol and drug abuse, seniors, children, housing, immigrant aid, and much more. Their contributions often go to groups that do not share their religious beliefs. While some are "poor as church mice," many are well endowed and capable of substantial contributions.

Usually, the clergy are so worried about raising money to repair the roof or meet the budget that they are not able to think about giving it away. You may get a more sympathetic hearing from the heads of outreach committees, women's groups, men's groups, youth groups, and religious educators.

Ask your board, volunteers and, if appropriate, the people you serve where they worship. If you get a donation from one place of worship, ask them to help you make contacts with others in the same denomination. Offer to send speakers to their meetings or services. Build a long-term relationship.

115

k. UNIONS

Many unions give money to charities and non-profit organizations. They are interested in social justice, services for seniors, health care, international development, and many other causes. Of course they will only support causes that they consider pro-union, so if you work with a large organization that is unionized, you have a better chance of getting a donation than if your management has tried to keep unions out. Unions also notice whether or not you have had your letterhead, business cards, or brochures printed in a union print shop. Union print shops can put a small union symbol, often called a "bug," on your printed material.

Document any work you do that would be of special interest to union members. Find a union member who supports your work to ask on your behalf. Then contact the largest or most progressive unions in your area. They may be listed in the phone book, often under "Labor." You may also contact the Labor Council in your area, which is an umbrella group for most unions. They may be able to provide a small donation and give you addresses and contact people at the most promising unions.

6

HOW TO APPROACH FUNDERS

Having developed your funding strategy, you now have a list of good prospects to approach. This chapter details the steps for approaching those prospective funders, focusing particularly on corporations because they are often the most difficult source fundraisers must tackle. However, much of what is covered can also be applied to approaching foundations, governments, and wealthy individuals.

a. ATTITUDE

If you hope to raise money from corporations but deep down inside you think they are corrupt, exploitive, many-headed monsters, chances are you won't meet with much success. As you learn more about the kind of decisions senior corporate people have to make, the risks they take, and the kind of jungle they compete in, your respect will grow.

One more note on attitudes. The presidential trappings of vast offices, fine art, and Persian rugs can be intimidating, especially if you have never before dealt with senior corporate management. It is useful to remember that the people you deal with, no matter how rich, brilliant, or powerful, are just people like you and me. They may not be ordinary, but they are people, and if you remember that, it helps you to say what you came to say.

b. SETTING UP A MEETING

It is very important to arrange a face-to-face meeting with the person in the organization who can do your cause the most

117

good. When you meet with someone, you become more than just another envelope full of worthwhile causes in need of more money. You become a person, an experience, and that personal contact can go a long way. You are probably more convincing in person than on paper.

1. Sneaking in through the front door

This means going directly to the source, such as the president of the company. It's worth your effort to try to see the president in the following situations:

(a) You are a controversial group and without the blessing of the president you won't get anywhere.

(b) Someone on your board or fundraising committee knows the president and can arrange an introduction for you.

(c) The corporation is very large and conservative and you have never approached them before.

The first challenge is get the president on the phone. That in itself is a task, because almost every president has a forward guard of secretaries to protect his or her valuable time. You have to be assertive and authoritative when you make that call. The secretary will answer and say "Ms. Black's office." You can be very formal and say "Yes, it's Joyce Young calling for Janet Black." If the president is actually there, the secretary may put you right through because you sound like you know the boss. If the president isn't there, the secretary will say, "I'm sorry, Ms. Black is in a meeting. May I have her call you?" DON'T LEAVE A MESSAGE BECAUSE SHE DOESN'T KNOW YOU AND WON'T CALL BACK. Say, "Thanks, but I'm going to be in a meeting shortly. When do you expect her back?" The secretary will tell you, and you make a note. Be sure to call back at that time.

If the secretary is especially friendly, you can try to get an appointment, but this usually doesn't work unless you already know the president or the secretary. Be nice to the secretary. She (it is still usually a woman) can decide whether or not you ever speak to the president. She may even have a lot of power to make decisions about grants. In a small company, she could even be the president's spouse! So learn her name, speak to her politely, and ask her to be your ally.

When you make this call, you have to be prepared to speak to the president and to convince him or her in three minutes to take the time to see you. So, in one sentence you have to say what your group does in a way that will impress, and in the next minute you have to show why he or she should be interested in what you are doing.

In response to your request for an appointment, the president may —

(a) make an excuse and try to put you off for a couple of months. Accept that, but if you get put off again, understand it as a polite "no." Either put your request to the president in writing or try to see someone else.

(b) suggest that you see somebody else. Unless you can come back with, "I particularly want to speak to you because you have been involved in such and such...," you will have to go along with the suggested substitute.

(c) say, "What you really want is money." Acknowledge that fact, but quickly add that you also value his or her perspective as a business person on such and such issue. Something like: "Yes, we do raise part of our funds from the corporate sector, but we especially seek the advice and perspective of the private sector on current social issues, especially child abuse, and that's why we want to speak to you. If you could give us half an hour of your time, I'm sure we can learn a lot from you."

Remember the fundraising adage:

IF YOU WANT MONEY, ASK FOR
ADVICE; IF YOU WANT ADVICE, ASK
FOR MONEY!

If you manage to speak to the president and you are quick on your feet during the phone call, chances of getting an appointment are fair to good. Be sure you are "up" and "focused" before you make this kind of call.

We've used the example of a corporate president, but the approach described in this section could be used for any senior official or for a wealthy individual.

2. The regular route

If you don't have cause to go see the president, or you can't get an appointment, you want to contact the person who handles donations. These people have various titles: "corporate affairs director," "corporate contributions administrator," "secretary to the donations committee," "chairperson of the contributions committee." Avoid the public relations department, however. They are more likely to evaluate your request as a marketing decision, not a philanthropic gift. Few small charities can truly offer corporate sponsors exciting results. For this discussion, we will use the example of a "corporate contributions administrator," or CCA.

The CCA is the secretary to the corporate contributions committee, if there is one. He or she is responsible for the initial weeding out process. The CCA assesses all the requests that come in (as many as 30 per day), chooses the ones that fit the company's areas of interest, and summarizes them on one or two pages for the committee to discuss and make decisions.

The committee is made up of three or more people from the company. If the company has defined certain areas of interest, they will try to find an in-house expert to serve on the committee. For example, if the company has a budget for funding the arts, somebody with interest and experience in the arts will be on the committee. A contributions committee will usually meet at least every six months and, in some cases, quarterly.

The CCA will make a verbal presentation and answer questions on the requests that made it to the committee level. That's why it is important to get to see the CCA and get him or her on your side.

To get the name of the CCA in an organization, phone the switchboard and ask, "Who handles donations to non-profit groups?" If the switchboard operator doesn't know, ask to speak to the director of public affairs. Most PR directors will be nice to you and quite patient because that's their job. Ask the PR director to whom you should address a request for funds. Get the correct spelling of that person's first and last name and their official title. Then write a one-page letter to the CCA introducing your organization and explaining that you would like to arrange a brief meeting to discuss such and such and you will call in a few days. Enclose your objectives sheet and annual report.

Don't enclose a funding proposal at this stage. You can introduce that topic at the meeting. In your approaches in the works log, note the letter, the date you mailed it, and the date you should phone back (see chapter 10).

c. THE MEETING

You've cleared the first hurdle: you've got a meeting with someone in the organization. Now, you need to prepare to make every minute in that meeting count for you.

1. Before the meeting

If you haven't already done so, read or skim the company's annual report. If your group has dealt with the company before, re-read the correspondence. If they have given you money before, know how much, when, what it was for, and the results of the work they funded. You want to have this information at the tip of your tongue.

Decide what information you want to get across and what information you want to get from them. Put a little scenario together in your head, and then be prepared to ad lib. Bring your objectives sheet and your annual report if you haven't already sent them. Don't put all the paper on the table when you arrive. Keep it in your briefcase, out of sight, unless the CCA asks for it. Focus on a conversation instead.

It is very important to take somebody with you to the meeting — a staff member, a board member — whoever is appropriate. You can be the business person and your partner can be the expert. That takes some of the pressure off you during the meeting, and it gives you somebody to compare notes with afterward. You should be able to communicate well with your fundraising partner so that the meeting will be a smooth, three-way discussion.

2. At the meeting

BE ON TIME! Punctuality is very important to corporate people.

Be appropriately dressed. Blue jeans or green hair aren't allowed when you are on their territory, and when you are asking them for money, you *are* on their territory. If you dress casually at work, it's a good idea to keep a suit, dress shoes, etc. in the office for short-notice meetings.

When your contact comes out to greet you, shake hands, introduce yourself, your organization, and your partner. Then begin the discussion. You might start by asking if he or she is familiar with your group, give a very brief history about how and why you were formed, and then get to the point — the project you would like funded. Try to get your listener involved and asking questions about your group. Encourage a real discussion and try to establish a rapport.

Keep an eye on your watch. If you said you only needed half an hour, get in and out in that space of time.

Should you discuss money in the meeting? Certainly you shouldn't discuss it until your meeting is almost over. Get your contact warmed up first. Don't discuss money at all unless you are comfortable, unless it feels right. Your contact assumes you are there to get money.

Be appropriately dressed.

If you don't know whether you've sold this person and you want to find out where you stand, try this approach:

"Before we go, perhaps you can tell us a bit about your areas of interest for funding. We are a registered charitable group, and we do depend on contributions from organizations like yours. Could you tell us the kinds of activities you fund and if you would be amenable to an approach for funding from our group?"

If you feel the person might respond to a very specific approach to fund a specific project, you might say "The total budget for our project is $40,000, which will cover salaries, travel expenses, and printing. We were considering asking your company for $4,000 toward our project. Would that be appropriate?"

In one fundraising effort, we were driving in the president's car back to his office after a superb luncheon at his private club. The president had commented on the power of positive thinking and expecting good results — cheerful and friendly chitchat.

President: "Well, I've really enjoyed talking to you, but I don't think you've put all your cards on the table. Don't you want to ask me for some money?"

Fundraiser: "We're not going to ask you for money, Don, we expect some money. The only question is how much!"

He burst out in laughter, but we got the money.

3. After the meeting

Immediately after the meeting, go have a cup of coffee with your partner, compare notes, and write down new ones. Summarize the discussion. Make a note of any requests for further information and questions or comments that were raised about your group. If the meeting was exploratory — not a specific approach for a specific project — decide what project or aspect of your activities you think that organization would like to fund and how much money they might contribute. Make some comments about your contact: "friendly and interested" or "bored and preoccupied." What kind of rapport did you establish with the CCA or the president? Were you on a first-name basis by the end of the meeting?

This list of information is called a profile sheet. It is worth doing because you won't remember all the details about that meeting, and next year when you or your successor approaches this source again, you will have some record of your relationship. Staple this to the inside of your file on the organization.

4. Back at the office

(a) Follow-up letter

When you get back to the office, or within a couple of days at the very most, write to the person with whom you met. Thank him or her for the meeting. Answer any questions or resolve any concerns that were mentioned. Add any new information relevant to your discussions. Introduce the funding proposal you enclose by reiterating the objective of the project in one paragraph. Mention the total budget and name the amount you would like them to contribute. For requests up to $1,000, a letter with your annual report and objectives sheet is all you need to send. Larger requests require a detailed funding proposal.

Should you name a price? Definitely. You should ask for a specific sum of money that you feel is fair. That removes a lot of guesswork for the donor. It makes the expectation clear. They can and will cut down your price if they think it's too high. Once a sponsor contributed $600 more than requested because they thought the project was under-budgeted. It was.

How much money you can expect one corporation to contribute depends on the following factors: the size of the corporation and its policies on contributions, the size of your group, how well known and established you are, how popular your cause is, and the nature and popularity of the project you are trying to fund. For instance, in a capital campaign, you can ask for much larger gifts than you can for an operating budget.

Some companies give in dribs and drabs (from $50 to $250) to a lot of groups. Other companies have a policy of giving to fewer groups in larger sums, from $1,000 to $4,000. A donation of from $1,000 to $4,000 from a large corporation to a project sponsored by an innovative or controversial group with an annual budget of $300,000 would be about par. That's a big generalization, but it will give you some idea what to expect. In the United States, many of the larger consumer-oriented corporations have defined specific areas of interest for funding and will give larger sums in those areas.

Many of the larger companies will require the approval of their board of directors for larger donations. That means it will take longer to get a decision on your request because you have to wait for a board meeting. That's the general climate for corporate giving to innovative group projects.

Foundations tend to give larger sums, from $4,000 to $10,000, if you approach the right one for your group. I can't generalize about government giving because it varies greatly depending on the agency and the kind of group you are.

(b) Keeping track

Enter the date of your letter and the amount you requested in your log (see chapter 10). If you don't hear from the organization within three months, call the person you dealt with and see how your request is coming. One good way to check is to call and say, "I'm planning my cash-flow for next month and I was wondering if we can count on a donation from (name of organization)." They understand cash-flow and will respond to it. If there is no decision yet, try to find out when they will make a decision, as this will indeed help you to plan cash-flow. Note any new information in your log.

d. WHAT TO DO WHEN A CHECK ARRIVES

When you are a fundraiser, you watch the mail like a hawk. On a good day you get a few checks or one big one. That *same day* you must write a nice letter confirming that you have received the check in the amount of $_____ and enclose their receipt. You can say a bit about the progress of the project they have funded and enclose copies of any recent press clippings about your group. Don't let this duty slip or get behind on it. The funders need that receipt to keep their accounting up to date. It's best if they get your thank-you letter before they get their canceled check.

Put the check in a safe place until you can get to the bank. Do this as soon as you record the check. Checks, like scraps of paper with phone numbers, can get lost. It's very embarrassing to have to contact the company and have them cancel and re-issue a check. Get into good habits about handling checks.

In Canada, you need to issue special tax credit receipts for donations. Businesses may not require you to issue a tax credit receipt, since they can deduct the donation as a promotional expense, whether or not your group is a registered charity. In fact, corporations never claim tax credits for half of all the receipts charities issue. You need an original plus one copy for each receipt. The receipts will have your charitable registration number and will be numbered sequentially. If you make a mistake in filling out a receipt, don't destroy it, just cancel it. The auditor will want to see it to make sure you aren't writing out receipts for yourself.

e. WHAT TO DO WHEN THEY SAY NO

If you are working hard, you will be getting "no" letters every other day. Don't tear up the "no" letter in anger and disgust. If you can't bear to read it closely, set it aside until later. It is important that you read these letters and learn from them.

In turning down your request, a corporation might say something like —

(a) "Your group does not fall within our mandate." (Get lost.)

(b) "We would really like to give you some money but we simply don't have any more." (Come back next year.)

(c) "Your group looks interesting but we are not able to fund you at this time." (We are waiting to see if your group will survive. Try again next year, earlier.)

Enter the "no" in your log and record it in your donations card file. Make a note of when you got a response. Since many companies only make decisions on requests once or twice a year, you don't want to miss the deadline next time.

Now sit down and write that company a letter. It may seem like an utter waste of time, but it's not. Sometimes you can find out why you were turned down without coming right out and asking. There must be no hint of sour grapes in this letter. You are just writing to say "Thank you for your consideration...this is what our group is up to and we will keep you informed of our activities." Why should you do this? It is a courtesy. The company will remember you for it. Sometimes it can help you really find out how that company regards your group. The times I did this it was worth its weight in information and rapport.

Don't let the "no's" depress you; they are part of a fundraiser's job. And don't give up on a source after one negative response. Unless you are clearly told to get lost, keep trying each year for three years before you give up. Keep that company on your mailing list.

f. THE OLD BUDDY ROUTE

Most of this chapter assumes that you, the fundraiser, are approaching the corporation yourself. You may have had a member of your board or fundraising committee help you get your foot in the door, but once you're in, you're on your own.

Rather than taking this approach, more traditional groups tend to rely heavily on the "old buddy system" approach. In that method, members of the board recruit other members of the business community to assist with soliciting corporations and wealthy individuals. These volunteers then directly approach their peers, the corporate presidents and vice presidents, and seek a contribution for your group.

With the old buddy route, the fundraiser's job is very different. The fundraiser does a lot of the work but is always behind the scenes. The fundraiser helps to identify and recruit fundraising volunteers, coordinates their approaches, provides the brochures, drafts follow-up and thank-you letters, and makes sure the tax receipt is sent.

If your group uses this approach for some of its fundraising, or if you are in a position to try it, here are a few words of advice.

Don't overload your volunteers; if you do, you'll lose them. The rule of thumb is that each volunteer should be given no more than five prospects to solicit.

Offer them some training in face-to-face fundraising. You can teach them how to do it and get them to organize their prospects in one four-hour session. It's a great morale booster too! See chapter 7 for an outline of a training session in face-to-face fundraising.

Be prepared to accept the judgment of your volunteer as to whether it is appropriate for him or her to approach a certain individual. If he or she doesn't feel comfortable about it, it won't work anyway. At the same time, you have to distinguish whether the volunteer is exercising good judgment or is just timid about asking. Nobody likes asking for money, and very few people find it easy.

Your volunteers are probably people of influence and affluence and, no doubt, very busy. Respect their time, use their time efficiently, and make it as easy as possible for them to do their end of the job.

Sometimes you will have fundraising volunteers who don't come through for you. They may put you off for months on end, promising and promising but never actually doing the job. Try a one-year rule: if a volunteer doesn't produce in the course of a year, look for a replacement.

The old buddy route for fundraising may not be acceptable or available to public interest groups. If your organization is in a position to use that approach, use your own judgment what would be acceptable and appropriate.

7

FUNDRAISING IN SMALLER COMMUNITIES

Matching wits with corporate presidents and trying to convince them to fund you is fine for groups located in big cities. But what if you are based in a small town?

If you live outside the major centers and you serve primarily the local community, your fundraising strategy and approach will be quite different. In this case, your potential base of financial support includes wealthy individuals in the community, local branch plants of major companies, support industries, local small businesses, members, and local government.

As a fundraiser in a small community, educating community leaders about philanthropy is an important part of your job. Try to speak on the topic of philanthropy at a chamber of commerce or business club luncheon. Make a case for the importance of charity, volunteerism, and giving. That investment of your time doesn't produce a quick return, but it usually pays off in the long run and it gives your group visibility.

a. INDIVIDUALS

Begin by identifying noteworthy individuals in the community — people of influence or affluence — who might be sympathetic to your cause. If your issues or activities are very controversial, this may be difficult or impossible. But you should at least try to identify some sympathetic influential people, and try to persuade them of the importance of your work. Like it or not, these people can affect not only your

131

success in fundraising, but your success in fulfilling your mandate.

Smaller cities and towns tend to have a small and clearly defined local establishment: the smaller the community, the greater the control exerted by this group. If you are able to get the local establishment or members of it to support your group, you will have a much easier time finding money and getting your program established. In that case, the best way to proceed with your fundraising will be through the "old buddy route" described in chapter 6. Because smaller communities are so tightly knit, fundraising peer pressure is all the more effective.

Here are a few basic principles for raising money from wealthy individuals. First, recruit as many "fundraising volunteers" as you can. These people will themselves be wealthy, prominent, respected members of the local establishment. They may be members of your board, or they may be volunteers recruited by your board. It is important that these individuals contribute financially to your group because they are then in a much better position to invite their friends and associates to contribute.

In a small-town setting, a fundraising committee structure would be effective. Committee meetings provide your volunteers with an opportunity to socialize and that makes their involvement more prestigious. If your fundraising volunteers end up competing with each other to see who can raise the most money, you're set! That won't happen if they never see each other.

Researching prominent families and individuals in the community will be your job. You need to identify those people who are capable of making a contribution in the dollar range you are seeking. Sources for your research include plaques on the walls thanking recent donors to hospitals, churches, community centers, colleges, recreation facilities, art galleries, park benches, tree planting, or any other past fundraising campaigns. These are people who are proven to be generous, and they are your best source.

Second best are people who are affluent, but may or may not be generous. To find them, research membership lists from golf clubs, country clubs, and the chamber of commerce, old-timers who know the life history of prominent families, and the local newspaper. The newspaper is a terrific source because in smaller towns a lot of the news is about people. You need to learn "who's who."

Try to get the largest contribution first. In the trade this is called "the pacesetting gift." If you can secure it first, you will have peer pressure working for you. Others in the community will want to donate in like measure. It will take a lot of work to get that first large gift, but that single donation might amount to 5% to 10% of your total budget, so it's worth it.

Remember that face-to-face solicitation is the most effective method for raising money from individuals. Telephone solicitation is the next most effective, and letter writing comes in a slow third. It is very important that prospective donors be approached by someone they know. The better they know each other, the better your chances of success.

Nobody likes asking for money and few people can build up the courage to do it often. For these reasons, you shouldn't expect your fundraising volunteers to solicit more than five prospects each, whether the prospects are individuals or corporations.

An important part of your job as a fundraiser is to build up the morale of your fundraisers so that they are confident about going door-knocking. You also have to be prepared to take a leadership role with your volunteers and encourage them to come through for you. Otherwise you are wasting your time, and so are they.

It is essential that you recognize and honor both your volunteers and individual donors. Volunteer and donor recognition can range from a sincere, personal thank-you letter, to a banquet honoring volunteers, to a hospice wing named after a generous donor. How you provide that all-important "thank-you" really depends on what would be fitting for your group, your volunteers, and your donors. Just be sure you do it on time and in good taste.

Although this is written in the context of fundraising in a small community, the principles for soliciting individuals apply anywhere.

b. TRAINING FOR FACE-TO-FACE FUNDRAISING

The following section outlines a two-hour training session to use with your board of directors, fundraising committee, or any other group you want to train in face-to-face solicitation. It teaches how to ask for money and uses role playing to develop confidence through practice. The greatest barriers are people's fear of asking for money and their fear of failure. The training described here is also useful for door-to-door fundraising and telephone fundraising or telemarketing.

1. Introduction

Open the session with some good news or a recent achievement of the organization. You might bring in a guest to talk about the importance of a new issue. Discuss something positive that will make the group feel motivated and involved.

Next, explain the overall fundraising program and how much you expect to raise from each sector, including individuals. Your volunteers need to see how they fit into the overall plan. Point out that approaching individuals is the fastest, easiest, and least expensive way to raise money. More than 80% of all charitable dollars raised in Canada and the United States each year comes from individual donations. Stress the need for your organization to raise funds from individuals.

2. Methods of solicitation

Ask the participants to recall times when they have been approached for a donation and answer the following questions:

(a) How were you approached?

(b) By whom?

(c) Where?

(d) When?

(e) Did you contribute?

(f) Why?

Have the group discuss their responses to each question. From this, each person will recognize how he or she responded to different types of solicitation. Talk about the effectiveness of the various approaches. Face-to-face is most effective, followed by telephone and letter, but many people are initially uncomfortable with face-to-face solicitation. By the end of the training session, most people will feel more comfortable about it, but if not, ask them to use the method that they can handle best. Each volunteer should use the fundraising method that he or she feels comfortable with. Better this than to lose them as fundraisers.

Participants should consider their own financial commitment to the organization. It's easier to ask for money if you are supporting the group financially yourself.

3. Dealing with fear

Ask how many people feel reluctant or afraid to approach somebody for money. Tell them to take a few minutes to think about that privately and to write down what they are afraid might happen. Then facilitate a group discussion about these fears. Don't pressure anyone to reveal what they wrote. Approach this discussion with an attitude of understanding and respect and stay away from pressure, guilt, or put-downs.

Simply having your volunteers identify and articulate their fears will go a long way toward resolving those fears. Some more experienced group members may say they used to feel that way too, but once they got out fundraising, they found their fears were groundless. The key is to help your volunteers work it through to a point where they are comfortable and ready to go. Once you get them talking honestly, it will be very clear what kind of support they need.

4. Three steps to approaching donors

Introduce your group to this three-step process in approaching potential donors: identify, inform, involve.

(a) Identify

Who would you think about approaching for money? The people most likely to give are current and past donors. Draw up this list:

(a) People who have made one or more unusually large donations.

(b) People whose total amount donated over the years is unusually high.

(c) People who have given much more frequently than most, even if their gifts are smaller. Include people who attend events.

(d) People whose total number of donations or length of time as a supporter over the years is unusually high, even if the total amount is not.

(e) People who give less than you think they could.

(f) People who give an odd amount of money, like $27 or $358. "An odd dollar amount," says Chicago fundraiser/author Joan Flanagan[1], "can be a clue the

---

[1] Joan Flanagan has written several excellent books, including: *Successful Fundraising: A Complete Handbook for Volunteers and Professionals, The Successful Volunteer Organization,* and *The Grass Roots Fund Raising Book,* Fitzhenry & Whiteside.

donor is allocating his or her total annual charity budget among several non-profits. This suggests the donor plans his or her charitable giving and your group is already on the short list of good organizations."

(g) People with titles and degrees, if donors on your lists are professionals such as doctors, lawyers, dentists, university professors, or accountants. Also short-list people who have important job titles at work, such as president, vice-president, or manager.

(h) People who live in upper-income neighborhoods. A second address for their winter or summer homes is a sign of potential.

(i) Supporters who are known to be affluent and/or celebrities. Scan your donor list for familiar names. Are there well-known people who have given you a donation — even a small one? Look for business leaders, authors, artists, athletes, politicians — any sort of celebrity. You may not know all the names. It may help to have one or two knowledgeable friends go over the list with you, in strictest confidence. If time allows, check *Who's Who*, the *Directory of Directors*, or similar books. (See Appendix.)

Now you have your short-list of top prospects. Ask your board and volunteers to go over this list. Their job is to find the five people who they feel most confident in approaching.

If there are other people your board and volunteers think are better prospects, discuss them. If there are not five people on this list the volunteers feel good about approaching, brainstorm an additional list, possibly from their personal contacts.

Ask current or past board members, senior friends, and volunteers for donations. Even if your board members aren't wealthy, getting their financial support will impress other donors.

It's not enough for board members to give their time. Their financial contributions show leadership, even if the amounts are not large. Their gifts begin the campaign with success, proving their commitment.

It is reasonable to expect board members to give a bigger portion of their income to the group where they sit on the board than to any other (with the possible exception of their place of worship).

People who use your services are prime potential donors in most, but not all, cases. Watch your lists for any who are already donors or volunteers. This is essential for groups in the arts, where audience members or families of young musicians are among the best supporters.

It is also key for religious groups, sports, education, and many health organizations. Even those who help poor people may find that clients feel greater self-respect when invited to contribute toward the cost of services. However, this may be a very low priority for some groups.

Studies have shown that people with ordinary incomes and lifestyles have given major donations. Major donors are not limited to the super-wealthy or the famous names. They do NOT even have to be what is commonly called rich.

The most generous donors to nonreligious activities in Canada are most typically:

- Age 30 or older
- Married, with children or with children who have left home
- From two-income families
- Professional or managerial occupation
- $50,000 annual household income
- University-educated
- Regular religious service attenders
- Donors to religious organizations

- Residents of Canada's prairie provinces
- Active in the community
- Members of at least two associations
- Volunteers

The two most important factors are religion and community involvement. The most generous donors to religious organizations are often:

- Age 60 or older
- Married, aged 30 to 50, with children
- Married, aged 40+, with no children
- Single, age 50+, with no children
- Two-income families
- Professional or managerial occupation
- Annual personal income of $40,000+
- University-educated
- Residents of Canada's Atlantic region
- Very religious
- Regular religious attenders
- Active in the community
- Members of at least two organizations

Part of identifying donors is to discover your web of contacts. Only after exploring your contacts should you consider approaching strangers.

Build a cold list based on research. Discover promising strangers among the following:

(a) Donors to similar organizations. Look in annual reports, programs at events, newsletters, and plaques.

(b) Neighbors of community groups. List owners and employees of nearby businesses by asking the Chamber of Commerce, City Hall, or business improvement councils. Find the more well-to-do residents from real estate agents, developers, and directories.

(c) People known for generosity. Watch the news, *Who's Who*, and other directories. Check the lists of donors to political parties.

(d) People who can't say no. Who you know is important. Many prospects will give to a charity they do not support because of the person who asks them. Similarly, business people often give to a customer's favorite charity to get more business.

(e) People who can benefit. Some people and businesses want public recognition. They may want to honor someone they love. Offer them benefits they cannot get otherwise.

Now you are ready to brainstorm with the board, volunteers, major donors, and staff. Kim Klein, publisher of the *Grassroots Fundraising Journal*,[2] suggests asking everyone to check address books or card files and put a check mark beside the name of anyone who might share their interest in the nonprofit group. Finally, ask them to note how much they would be willing to ask for.

Ken's firm developed a webbing exercise that reveals your hidden network of connections: people you didn't know you knew. Get people to delve into themselves to uncover long-lost connections to people now in a position to provide help. Even when you do not have direct contacts with prospective major donors, you may know someone who knows someone.

The categories of potential donors below should spark some ideas for you when identifying donors. Those with asterisks (*) are types of people that research shows to be particularly generous:

- Accountants (self-employed)*
- African Americans*

[2] P.O. Box 11607, Berkeley CA 94712

- Association members
- Automotive industry
- Banks*
- Beverage industry
- Big companies
- Clients/customers of this non-profit; companies I know; other people in this field
- Clubs
- Colleagues
- Community leaders
- Doctors*
- Dentists*
- Donors to this group*
- Donors to other groups*
- Employers (past/present)
- Entertainment industry
- Family
- Farmers*
- Food distributors/producers
- Foundations
- Friends
- Hospitality industry
- Insurance
- Land developers
- Law
- Local businesses
- Media
- Medicine
- Neighbors
- Nurses

- Oil and gas
- Older people
- People you met recently or long ago
- Politicians
- Pharmaceuticals
- Places of worship
- Printing
- Professions
- Publishing
- Real estate
- Religious people*
- Retailers
- Seniors*
- Service clubs
- School friends
- Small business*
- Sports
- Suppliers to companies I know; other suppliers to non-profit groups; suppliers in this field
- Textiles
- Transport
- Trust companies*
- Unions
- University-educated*
- Volunteers*

(b) Inform

How could your participants inform the people on their list about your group?

(a) Pass on a newsletter or press clipping?

(b) Sell raffle or dance tickets?

(c) Invite to an open house?

(d) Mention your involvement in a conversation?

Participants should write down one appropriate thing they could do to inform each of the five people.

(c) Involve

How could your volunteers involve these people? The reaction volunteers receive to the informing step is your best clue. If people aren't interested, they should be left alone. If they are interested, asking them to contribute or asking them to volunteer is a logical next step.

5. Playing the role

Have participants form groups of three: a fundraiser, a prospect, and an observer. Ask them to improvise and act out a solicitation for ten minutes. They should select an appropriate circumstance and act accordingly.

Avoid restaurants. There are too many distractions and social graces to worry about, and deciding who pays is awkward. Also, avoid asking for money at parties. But if you do happen to meet a possible donor at a function, Joan Flanagan suggests that you make polite conversation, trying to listen and learn as much as possible about the prospect. The next day, send your prospect a brief letter — one paragraph on how much you enjoyed meeting him or her and one paragraph on how you would like to have an opportunity to tell more about your project. Include one recent clipping and one brochure. Send a copy of your letter to the host or hostess with your thanks for making the introduction.

When volunteers make an appointment to approach a real donor, they must indicate that they want to discuss their volunteer work. Don't pretend that it is a purely social call, hoping to sneak up on the subject. If the potential donor would refuse to see you knowing that this is a fundraising call, cultivate the relationship first. Don't rush.

In the meeting, after a small amount of socializing, participants should go into their pitch and carry it through without going off on major tangents. In their scenarios, volunteers should follow these steps:

(a) Mention the organization, their role in it, and some detail about why they became involved and what they do there. They should let their feelings about the organization show; sincere emotion lends weight to words.

(b) Describe the organization, what it does, and why they think it is important. They should say what it does that makes them proud to be involved.

(c) Outline the group's budget and what parts of it need to be raised from individuals. They can mention a specific project they are trying to raise money for.

(d) Ask their friend to help out this organization by making a financial contribution.

(e) Name a specific dollar amount which they think is appropriate for their friend to donate.

(f) Stop talking, smile, and wait for their friend to react. If he or she asks a question, they should answer it briefly, then ask for the dollar amount again.

(g) After they receive the money or a check, they should ask if the donor wants a receipt for tax purposes. Volunteers should have receipts and brochures on hand, if possible.

(h) Thank the donor, and say how this contribution will help their group.

After this enactment, have the observer and the prospect give the fundraiser feedback about what was effective and what wasn't. When the whole workshop regroups, initiate a discussion about what was effective and what wasn't. Ask what was hardest, and how they felt.

6. Action

Have each volunteer decide which five people he or she will approach, how, when, and where. These names should be put before the whole group so there will not be duplication. Set a date when the committee will meet again to report its results. This will boost follow-through.

7. Follow-up

Call your volunteer fundraisers to see if they have approached their friends and how it went. Provide support and coaching. Praise the successful ones; encourage those who are shy or tardy.

c. LOCAL MAJOR INDUSTRY

Often smaller cities are dominated by one major industry and this situation can cause problems for the fundraiser. There may be only a few companies that you can approach for a substantial donation.

If your local major corporations are subsidiaries or branches with head offices in a major center, you may face a second problem: the local industry may have a very small regional donations budget, or no budget at all. In some cases the local manager (or franchise owner) has authority to make small donations without requesting permission from head office. These are usually up to $500. Bank branches, supermarkets, retail stores, restaurant franchises, and gas station chain outlets are just a few examples. These may be part of a big business, but they want to have a hometown feeling.

The larger donations budget would be allocated by head office. It's also quite possible that the local general manager needs head office approval for donations over a few hundred dollars. On the other hand, there may be a growing tendency for industries to strengthen local donations budgets

— companies become decentralized and make larger contributions in the "company" town. Certainly in head-office/branch-plant operations the management trend is toward greater local autonomy, and this applies throughout government and business.

Your first task is to approach the general manager and convince him or her of the importance of your group. If you have a fundraising friend who can make this approach for you or with you, so much the better.

In your meeting, ask what the company's policy is regarding donations to local groups from both the regional budget and the head office budget. Try to persuade the general manager that it would be good public relations for the company to increase its donations budgets in the communities where it operates. Give whatever support, ideas, and ammunition you can for getting more of the company's charitable dollars into your community. Unfortunately, in a national company, the head office budget is often allocated to national groups. In that case you will have to settle for what you can get from the regional budget.

If that's not the case, or if the general manager isn't entirely certain how it works, try to get him or her to work with you to approach head office for a contribution. Here's the best way to do this.

After you have met with the general manager, follow up with a two-page letter explaining what your group does, what you need the money for, how much you need, and why that particular company should contribute. Try to get the manager to make a commitment from the regional budget.

Ask the manager to forward your request together with a covering letter to head office. The covering letter should say why the manager thinks you are a good group, why head office should contribute, and how much they should give. In other words, you convince the local manager, he or she donates, and then convinces the head office to give also.

It may be that the general manager takes a very dim view of your group and has turned you down before. Should you try to approach head office directly? In most cases the answer is no because the people at head office are going to be very, very reluctant to go over the head of the local manager on a local matter. In fact, head office might well send such a letter back to the general manager to draft a reply! Then the general manager will take an even dimmer view of your group.

Matching employee contributions is the other common technique for soliciting local major industries. For every dollar you raise from the company's employees, the company contributes the same amount or, perhaps, twice as much. Often such a scheme is in place for well-established charities, but it won't automatically apply for your group.

To set up a matching employee contributions scheme, approach the union leadership first. The union leadership will be much more effective than you in soliciting its membership and persuading management to match employee contributions. Once you persuade the union leadership to support you, try to get the company's agreement to match the funds. Get this before you solicit the union membership. The members will feel that their donation is accomplishing more if they know it will be matched by the company.

d. LOCAL SMALL BUSINESS

The industrial base in your community may consist of many small industries and businesses. You may find plant managers and independent proprietors who have little or no experience with philanthropy. Outside of political contributions and a yearly gift to the United Way (if you have one), they may have never even been approached before. They won't have a specified donations budget, let alone funding committees, policies, and areas of interest.

147

To solicit local small business and industry, you could either use the old buddy route or try going yourself. The "go yourself" approach might work with the owners of small business because they are entrepreneurs, and they will admire initiative.

In the United States, a lot of the corporate giving is done at the local level in the form of $200 to $500 donations. Cultivate this source because once you get on the list, it's renewable money.

e. SPECIAL EVENTS

Charity art sales, auctions, swim-a-thons, raffles, concerts, fundraising dinners — all of these activities are fundraising special events. They tend to be popular methods of raising funds in smaller towns and cities. In some places, a special event is the only form of fundraising people know.

Special events can be an effective vehicle for promoting your group, getting publicity, and broadening your volunteer base. They are not always the most efficient method of fundraising. These activities are very labor intensive, they require money to initiate, and they can burn out your volunteers. Women's committees and auxiliaries in particular tend to put an enormous amount of work into this form of fundraising with little financial outcome.

The point is this: be clear about your own objectives and recognize special events for what they require and what they achieve. If your top priority is to raise money, your time might be better spent soliciting individuals.

1. General principles

There are two key requirements for a successful special event. You need a large and active group of volunteers to do the work. You need the kind of event that you know will appeal to your membership and the community at large.

The success of many community-based fundraising events depends on people. You need good people, and enough of them, to make it work. You need people who are organizers and leaders, people who do the different volunteer jobs, people who come to the event and spend money. Some special events take more people than others. Make sure you have the people to do the job. Remember, too, that organizing a fundraising event may be a good way to interest new people — people who have never been involved before — in joining your group.

Check whether you can afford to hold the event. If you are having a concert or holding a dance, for example, you need to pay out the expenses before you collect the income. If you don't have any "up front" money to spend, certain events will be impossible for you.

Before you decide to go ahead with a fundraising event, try to calculate how much money you will make from it. Figure out exactly what your expenses will be, and then estimate how much money will come in from the event. When you subtract your expenses from the revenues, you get profit.

For example, if you are holding a raffle, write down the names of all the people who will sell tickets and how many tickets each person will sell. Try to get each person to agree to sell a certain number of tickets: give each person a quota. Figure out the total number of tickets that will be sold, multiply that by your cost per ticket, and that will give you your total revenue. Then subtract your expenses, for printing the tickets, etc. and you will have your profit.

Some fundraising events generate more money for less work than others. You will only find out which methods are "most profitable" in your community by experimenting and keeping careful records. It's important to compare different events to see how much money you make for how much work. People like variety, so you may need to keep trying new kinds of events to keep people coming out.

Try to get everything donated. If it's an auction sale or bake sale or raffle, try to get everything you sell donated. Sometimes you can't avoid expenses, for example when you have a concert or show a movie. As a general principle, you should try to get things donated.

Hold several money-making activities at the same time. If you are showing a movie, you might try selling tickets for a raffle at the door and sell popcorn, drinks, cookies, T-shirts, and posters at a concession stand. If you are having a concert, you might have a break and hold a dance contest where people pay to enter the contest and there is a prize. It takes a lot of work to get people to come out to an event, so once you have them out you want to give them a lot of different ways to spend money!

If you want to sell T-shirts or buttons, remember economy of scale: the more you have made up at one time, the less each one costs you. The lower your costs, the greater your profits. Therefore, if you can get a large quantity of T-shirts printed at once, it will be more profitable for you. But don't get more made than you feel sure you can sell!

Pay a lot of attention to the timing of the event. You don't want your date to conflict with major sports events or other local attractions.

2. Types of events

The following is a list of ideas, tips, and warnings on how to successfully organize three common events: a film night, an auction, and a dance or concert. Many of the tips will apply to other types of events as well.

(a) Film night

Get the free film rental catalogues offered by companies who rent 16 mm films or videos. Order your films several months ahead in case there are any transportation problems. You don't want people to show up and find out that your film is lost in the mail. Planning early will also give you a lot of opportunity to promote the film on radio and put up posters. About a week before the film night, get someone to review the film on radio or TV. This will generate more interest.

When the film comes in, preview it. Run the film or video once to make sure that the technology is working and there are no tears in the film. Be sure to have an extra projector bulb on hand, just in case. Get somebody who knows a lot about the technology to act as your volunteer "projectionist."

Get volunteers to make popcorn, brownies, cookies, and buy some juice or soft drinks in bulk to sell at the concession stand during intermission. Set the prices so that you will make some profit. The concession stand can be a good money-maker, especially if you have good food and you are running a double feature!

Insure the film for its return journey: if it gets lost in transit the film dealer can charge you for the cost of a new print.

(b) Auction

Before you decide to have an auction, check around to see if people have things to donate, and look for some inexpensive clothing to sell. Make sure you have enough items to make a good auction.

Among the most lucrative objects to auction are fantasy items, where the value is not restricted by marketplace costs. These include unique experiences, nostalgia, and/or celebrities.

The following are examples:

(a) Dinner cooked by a volunteer fire fighter who has a talent in the kitchen, and served by a local celebrity like the mayor.

(b) A day of gardening by someone with a green thumb.

(c) A ride in a hot air balloon, perhaps owned by a local brewery, pizzeria, or real estate company.

(d) A week in a private cottage, a city apartment, or on a boat, donated by someone who will be away.

Here are a few real-life examples of celebrity items that have raised money for charities:

(a) A walk-on part on "Seinfeld" fetched $15,000 at a rain forest charity auction.

(b) Pete Rose's good-behavior voucher from an Illinois minimum-security prison raised $770.

(c) The Toronto Humane Society's dinner and auction raised about $38,000, including items donated by Betty White, Elizabeth Taylor, and other celebrity animal lovers.

Get a good auctioneer — somebody who is funny and not shy — somebody who will give the audience a good time. Radio and TV personalities will often do this. Politicians are also good volunteers who are used to both public speaking and fundraising.

Put starting prices on the larger or more valuable items, to make sure somebody doesn't buy a couch for 50¢ just because nobody else wants it. A "reserve bid" keeps items from selling too cheaply. For art work, the artist may be offended if people appear not to value the art highly. But do not show the normal retail value of the item; this encourages bargain hunters to stop bidding below the retail price, which becomes the maximum bid.

Be imaginative about what you can sell. Crafts, art work, pies, jams, and preserves can be auctioned. Besides selling things, you could sell a ride on somebody's new boat, a music lesson or a poetry lesson, a diet dinner, a date, the first peek at a new baby, six weeks of yoga lessons — whatever you can think of and people will agree to.

Organize a food concession and bake sale to be held the day of the auction. Always charge a small admission fee to the auction — if people don't want to pay an entry fee, they are not the sort who will make your auction a success by bidding high.

Be sure to have somebody write down who bought what for how much. It's handy to do a list of the items and give each item a number and then sell them in order. Set the items out at least an hour ahead of auction time so that people have a chance to look at them up close before the sale starts.

Organize the cashier carefully so that the lineup to pay at the end of the sale won't take too long. Make a little card for each person's name. When the cashier gets the sheet of who bought what, he or she should write on that person's card what they bought and for how much. Then, when a person comes to pay, the cashier just adds up that person's card. Be sure to get a full mailing address and phone number for each person who attends, so you can approach them in the future for a straight donation.

(c) Dance or concert

Get good entertainment. It may not be possible to attract famous groups to come and play because it might be too expensive, but if a few communities get together to book a tour by a band, and if the band is interested in seeing your part of the country, it might work out.

As mentioned above, consider adding a dance contest or, at the least, a concession to bring in more money.

(d) The no-event event

Hold a non-event and invite people to stay at home! This tried-and-true technique is sometimes called a No-Tea Tea, or a Dinnerless Dinner. WARNING: this does not work if your people are party animals.

Tell people how much you save by not renting a hall, arranging catering, and hiring a band. All the money they give goes to good works.

Remind them how much they save by not hiring a baby-sitter, getting their hair done, buying party clothes, and paying for parking. Attach a tea bag (donated of course) to the ticket and encourage the donors to throw their own tea party.

You can send clever invitations announcing a non-reception, not to be held anywhere, followed by people not scheduled to perform. Send reply cards with a note like the following:

GEE, THANKS FOR LETTING ME STAY HOME.

Here's my contribution to ensure that I will be invited NOT to attend again next year!

☐ $15 I will not attend.

☐ $25 Neither I nor my companion will attend.

☐ $50 No member of my family will attend.

☐ $100 I will keep the neighbors away.

☐ $250 I will keep my politician away.

☐ $ _____ I will have my own party.

8

DIRECT MAIL

With the direct mail method of fundraising, groups solicit funds from individuals by sending them a letter in the mail. To do this you require a strategy, a mailing list, a package, and some money.

Think through your direct mail campaign very carefully before you launch it. Figure out the cost of the mailing, and the percentage of success required to break even and to make a profit. Direct mail has become extremely popular in the past decade, and many seasoned fundraisers feel the market is saturated. However, if the package is good and the issue and timing are right, direct mail still boasts a good enough response rate to make it worth considering.

However, direct mail has become harder in the last few years. More people are throwing mail away without opening the envelope. Costs are rising and response rates are plummeting. It can still be effective, but a few of the rules have changed. More than ever, a non-profit has to know what works and what doesn't.

a. STRATEGY

It is best to use a direct mail campaign for a specific issue that is high-profile, easily understood by the general public, and compelling. A "cold letter" (a letter to an individual you have never contacted before), asking for a contribution to your operating expenses is pretty boring, and will quickly land in the garbage. However, a letter asking for money to house the homeless, protect abused children, or save a scenic gorge is something everybody can relate to. In other words, emotional issues with broad appeal or high-profile political issues — issues most people are aware of or affected by — are most likely to bring in direct mail money.

Direct mail has an annual cycle: your campaign has a better chance at certain times of the year. Summertime is generally poor because people are on holiday. September to November is the best time, and February to June is the next best time to do your campaign. Mailings a month or two before Christmas will do very well.

b. THE MAILING LIST

Once you have focused on an issue that has the right characteristics, you have to identify a target group that is sensitive to this issue and can afford to contribute.

If you wanted to raise money for an inner-city playground, you might want to focus on parents and teachers. When you have your target group, you will know what kind of mailing list you want and can begin to look for a list or lists that will serve your need. For the example above, you might try to get a home and school association list, a teachers' federation list, or rent the list from a children's magazine.

It is common and accepted practice for groups to exchange their mailing lists for a one-time use. Although it may sound suspicious at first, experience has shown that both groups keep their existing donors and gain new ones this way. Put all the details in writing because any misunderstanding about the use of another group's mailing list is hard to overcome after the fact.

In large cities, you can also rent lists from direct mail brokers who make it their business to keep and build lists that are very specific. This increases the cost of your campaign because renting a mailing list will cost anywhere from $75 to $150 per thousand names, depending on the list.

Try to build your own mailing lists. When you attend a conference, get the conference mailing list. When you are invited to speak to a gathering of people, you can circulate an attendance record. Ask people to write their names, addresses, and phone numbers and indicate their special interests and whether they would like to receive more information on your group. When people phone or write to you for information or order a publication, get their names and addresses. Since these people have already been exposed to your group, you have a better chance of getting money from them.

Sometimes, established groups in your field will send out your fundraising letter with their regular mailing to their membership. This is called "piggy-backing" your mailing. There is a limit on how often an established group can do this as they don't want to exploit their membership. For a very special issue or an emergency, you might try approaching a group with a large membership for this favor.

c. THE PACKAGE

The package is what you put in the mail. There must be four key pieces:

(a) The letter

(b) The reply card

(c) A self-addressed postage-paid envelope

(d) An interesting exterior envelope

1. The letter

This letter must be one of the best letters you write. Make it as personal as possible. If the person has donated to you before, or you are asking for a big donation, the person's name should be added by computer using mail merge. It can even be written in by hand. This may also be practical for a small mailing. It is not usually economically justifiable for mailings of several thousand, but that may change as the cost of computer work continues to go down and the cost of postage increases. Have the letter done on a word processor that can produce many original letters but changes the name on each one. You need software with a mail-merge function to do this.

The letter should be signed personally, or it can be signed by a famous person who supports your group. People who delve into the psychology of direct mail even know what kinds of names are most effective and will sign a good-sounding fictitious name to a fundraising letter. That's a bit extreme in our view.

The letter should be two pages, or maybe four or more. Contrary to common belief, a one-page letter does not raise more money — it almost always raises less. While people protest that they are too busy to read long letters, the real issue is not length but interest. People will skip over a five-word newspaper headline if they are not interested but will stay up late reading a 300-page book that they just can't put down. We are not suggesting a 300-page letter, but do take two pages or four pages or even more to tell an exciting human interest story that will engage people's hearts. It should speak directly and personally to the target group. A clear and simple description of what you want the money for and a background paragraph or two on your group are required.

At the end of your letter comes the clincher asking for the money. You might say: "If you contribute $50, that will help preserve another Dead Elm and the baby woodpeckers that make it their home. Of course, anything you can contribute will help and will be appreciated."

When you are using figures in a letter the amount looks like less if you don't use the cents column. It's just a trick of the eye, but $50.00 at first glance looks larger and therefore more intimidating than $50 does. The same sales technique suggests using a figure like $695 rather than $700, though you may not want to use such tactics for your campaign.

Sample #9 is an example of a simple yet effective direct mail letter.

2. The reply card

The reply card gives the donor the opportunity to write on something saying, "I have contributed." In the trade, this is called "interactive marketing."

Keep track of your responses by coding the reply card. For example, if you were doing an experimental direct mail campaign in the Toronto area, you would mail to 1,000 homes in each of Rosedale, Forest Hill, Mississauga, Markham, and Richmond Hill. (The wisdom of the trade is that you need to mail at least 5,000 pieces to get a meaningful test.) Code your reply cards: R for Rosedale, F for Forest Hill, M for Mississauga, and so on. When you analyze the return results, you will know where there is the most interest and decide where to focus your next campaign.

The reply card also lets you ask for a specific dollar range of contribution. The choices can range from $25 to $500 and include an "other" category. You can also ask one or two survey-type questions or promote a product on the reply card, but don't overdo it. For one example of a reply card, see Sample #10.

3. The reply envelope

It's always a good idea to enclose a self-addressed, business reply envelope. The return envelope makes it that much easier for the donor to drop a check in the mail. The extra work and expense of a business reply envelope will be repaid with a higher return on your mailing.

Business reply envelopes that are postage-paid are expensive, but not as expensive as you may think. It generally increases the reply rate and the average donation, so it is a good investment. One common practice is to provide the reply envelope and let your donor pay the postage. However, this does not produce such good results. Many people cannot

Canadian Crossroads International
Carrefour Canadien International

November 18, 199—

Dear Friend,

Unless our computer has goofed again, your name came up along with 758 others when I asked it for people who had contributed to Crossroads in 1992 or 1993 but not in 1994. What really astonished me was when I asked the computer how much you folks had collectively contributed. It was $47,000! That's a BIG chunk out of our budget and explains why we are so far behind on our fund raising goals this year at CCI.

You and I don't want to see CCI face its first deficit ever. Your gift is **really needed** between now and December 25th to help us avoid a deficit.

You know that CCI has been facing alternatives which many of us find unpleasant - such as looking at major program diversification, being forced to cut back aspects of our program which we believe are fundamental to our quality. The volunteers of the national fund raising committee believe that we can avoid some of these sacrifices if we all pull together and give Crossroads our financial support.

We are looking at ways to help CCI on a long-term basis as well - such as establishing a planned giving program through which our donors can leave a gift in their will to CCI which will be put into a permanent endowment fund to benefit CCI forever. As you can imagine, such gifts build up quickly and can make a major difference in determining whether CCI will be able to carry on into the 21st century.

We have been working very hard to improve our data base. For this reason, we are sending you with this letter a questionnaire which we would ask you to take a few minutes to fill out. This will help us to ensure that our data is accurate and to provide good service to you.

In the holiday season, we all give to many worthy causes. Please take a few minutes to write a cheque to CCI and BE GENEROUS!. **The only group that CCI can truly count on is its past supporters.** A $47,000 shortfall is a big one for us to face. Your gift - big or small - makes a BIG difference to us. It allows CCI to maintain quality programming and to continue to work to ensure that Canadians have experiences which promote a world of understanding - a world in which there is less racism, less hatred, less inequality.

SAMPLE #9 — Continued

James Robinson said that "The world changes one person at a time". We have seen a lot of positive changes in the world in recent years - the taking down of the Berlin Wall, the end of the Cold War, the beginnings of a fragile peace in the Middle East, a black majority government in South Africa. Yet, literally billions of the world's citizens continue to live in terrible poverty. Children die on a daily basis from malnutrition and disease.

You and I both know that it is more important than ever to provide a way for Canadians to come to grips with the realities of our complex world. We need leaders who can understand the cultures and peoples from around the world. We need Canadians who are sensitive to the conditions which exist in developing countries. *We need Canadians who are prepared to fight racism and hatred in their daily lives.* Crossroads has been responsible for providing personal growth experiences to a whole host of Canadians and Crossroaders from developing countries. It has built thousands of tiny bridges across the gaps of racism and hatred which separate humanity.

We need to ensure that such bridges will continue to be built in future. **Think for a moment about the impact CCI had on your life or on the lives of people you know.** You know it was an important impact. You know that Crossroads deserves to continue to do its good work. Let us know by your gift that you care about the objective of creating a world of understanding. Your gift is crucial to that objective. Crossroads needs YOUR SUPPORT MORE THAN EVER.

Thank you in advance for your past support and for your help and suggestions. The future of CCI is in our hands. Let's fight to maintain an organization that has PROVEN WORTH - Canadian Crossroads International.

Yours sincerely,

Harry

Harry Qualman
Coordinator, National Fund Raising &
Crossroader from 1961

P.S. Please consider the possibility of joining our club of monthly givers, the James Robinson Society with even a small monthly gift. AND PLEASE, return the questionnaire! Thanks.

Also, if by any chance your gift came in the mail while this letter was going out, please note this on your questionnaire and excuse our error.

STOP THE CRIES OF TORTURE...

I want to help save the lives of men, women, and children detained in prison, tortured, or executed because of their political or religious beliefs.

I'm enclosing my tax creditable donation of:

☐ $25 ☐ $35 ☐ $50 ☐ $100 ☐ $150 ☐ Other $_____

Kelly Smith
123 Oak Avenue
Woodville, Ontario
M3G 1T5

In addition to my financial contribution, please send me information about membership in AI. ☐

AI occasionally exchanges names of supporters with other non-profit organizations. If you do not wish to receive information from groups other than AI, please indicate here: ☐

Amnesty International 130 Slater Street, Suite 900, Ottawa, Ontario K1P 6E2 quickly find a stamp at home, and by the time they do, their commitment to write your cause a big check may have cooled off. Contact the post office for information on postage-paid envelopes.

If you decide to use postage-paid envelopes and you are doing a large enough mailing, you can apply for a business reply mail number from the post office. It may take a few weeks, so don't wait until the last minute to apply. With a reply mail number, you don't have to waste money on stamps: you will only be charged postage for the reply envelopes that are used by donors. Both the Canadian and American postal systems have business reply mail numbers, but these numbers cannot be used for a mailing that is going out of the country and there are other requirements. The post office is the best source of information on this.

Go to a printer and have envelopes printed with your address and the business reply mail number. Make sure that these envelopes fit inside the envelopes you will be using for sending out the whole package. Get extra ones printed at the same time. The cost of printing envelopes drops rapidly with volume. You can use the extras in future mailings. Tuck them into newsletters, annual reports, and brochures. The more you hand out, the more money you will raise.

The envelope may be the single most important part of the package. If people throw the package away without opening the envelope, it does not matter if your letter is sincere or brilliant — people won't see it. Here are some tips that apply to letters to individual supporters in their homes, not to organizational donors in their offices.

The envelopes that are opened most rapidly have a real, live stamp, not a printed permit or a postage meter. Special commemorative stamps are better than the regular ones. Unfortunately, these cost more and are more difficult to apply by machine, so more organizations can't do this except for small mailings to their most important individual donors.

A hand-written address is also more personal, and more likely to be opened. Again, this is possible only for small quantities. Second best is an envelope with the donor's name and address typed (or laser printed) right on the envelope. For large volumes, most organizations settle for a window envelope with the donor's name and address on the reply card — this makes it easy for them to reply, and you can be sure that the name and address match your original list. Avoid sticking a mailing label on the exterior envelope. This not only looks like junk mail, it lacks the convenience.

The great debate is whether or not to add a "teaser." This is a phrase or artwork designed to capture the reader's interest. Sometimes a completely blank envelope will work, but usually people balance their curiosity about the contents with their anger at too many solicitations. If your cause is popular, the name of your group may be enough. If you have the support of a celebrity, his or her name and/or photo may do the job, or it might look like another sweepstake. If you work with kids, their artwork may work well. A few words that ask an intriguing question or state a startling fact might do the trick.

Whatever your solution, work hard on the envelope, don't just leave it to the last moment as an afterthought. Make sure the envelope and the letter are consistent. Test a few to find which style works best for you.

d. COST-BENEFIT ANALYSIS

In Canada, a 0.5% response rate is not unusual for a prospect mailing to acquire new donors, a 1% response is good, and 2% or 3% is very good, and over 3% is fantastic. That is the rule of thumb, but it varies according to the strength of your strategy, your list, your package, and the locale. It also depends, of course, on the dollar amount of the donations from the respondents. If you get a 3% response but the checks are small, you might just break even.

When you plan your fundraising campaign budget, plan to break even financially with a small response on a donor acquisition mailing. By breaking even, we mean recovering the actual cost of the mailing, not including labor. You should be using volunteer labor.

In the United States, the direct mail situation is quite different. Some groups feel that the market is saturated and say it takes two years to begin to break even with "prospect mailings," the mailings where you try to capture new donors. For the first two years, you have to re-invest all the income in the direct mail program itself. If you are thinking about getting into direct mail, assess it carefully, and consider it a long-term proposition.

Certain categories of tax-exempt U.S. groups get subsidized postage rates for second and third class mail. Inquire about a third class non-profit mailing permit at your local post office.

Canadian postage rates offer a complex array of discounts depending on the number of pieces you mail, the size of the envelope, the weight of each unit, the postal code order you sort the envelope, and where you drop off the mailing. Unfortunately there is no discount for charities. Consult one of Canada Post's special direct mail representatives for assistance.

The cost-benefit analysis is different for mailing to people who have already given you a donation at least once. This is much more effective than the donor acquisition mailings discussed above, otherwise there would be no point in doing donor acquisition in the first place. For every hundred you mail out, you should expect at least 20 to 40 donations. If the letter is very exciting, you might even get 60 replies. However, that still means from 40% to 80% of your proven supporters have *not* sent a contribution.

To get more of them to give, ask more often. You may have just reached them on a bad day. Another mailing might reach them when they feel generous. Good mailing campaigns go to proven donors much more than once a year. Send fundraising requests at least three or four times a year. Write more often if your cause deals with a situation that changes rapidly, or if your group handles many different issues, or if your organization really needs money urgently. Many groups successfully mail seven to twelve times a year.

Some donors, inevitably, request that you send them letters only once a year. Most donors need several reminders just to give once. Many will give more than once a year, if you catch their interest.

Within two or three weeks of sending a mailing, you will know how successful you have been. If nothing arrives in the first three weeks, your mailing has been unsuccessful. About 50% of the total response will come in during those first three weeks. After that, a few checks may dribble in slowly.

You can increase your return by doing telephone follow-up to those in your locale who have not responded. A simple call from a volunteer saying, "Did you receive our letter?" or "Can we count on your contribution?" will improve your return. (See the next chapter.)

e. SUMMARY

Direct mail can be a very effective fundraising tool when used by the right group for the right issue. When you have to raise funds for an emergency such as a court case, or you need money to repay a deficit, direct mail can play an important role. It is, however, expensive in materials and labor. It is also a high-risk form of fundraising because the initial investment is high. Just be sure you have thought it all through before you make the investment. To be successful, direct mail requires a special savvy — knowing who your target group is, what turns them on, and how to motivate them to reach into their pocketbook. Direct mail can bring in a huge amount of income, even after the considerable expenses. The real payoff, however, comes from up-grading these direct mail donors. Ask them to give more than last year, give more than once a year, give monthly, have donations automatically deducted from their checking account, credit card, or paycheck, or get their employer to match the contribution.

9

TELEPHONE FUNDRAISING

Telephone fundraising has a bad name. Too many people have been irritated by annoying calls. The phone always seems to ring when you are in the shower, at dinner, or changing a crying baby's diaper. Sometimes the call is about a cause you never heard of before. Worst of all are the robot-like voices of weary callers reading a boring script for the hundredth time, or the over-aggressive callers who won't take no for an answer. In some cases, phone canvassers are actually fraudulent.

Nevertheless, telemarketing can be effective in certain circumstances.

a. WHEN DOES TELEPHONE FUNDRAISING WORK?

The telephone can be more effective than other forms of communication. For instance, it is a cost-effective way to renew the support of lapsed or past donors who have not responded to letters. Reply rates can be five times better than mail, and average donations are two or three times higher.

When calls are made to your current supporters, the telephone is one of a number of reliable techniques to increase their giving. When funds are needed to cope with an emergency, or a major breakthrough needs to be announced, the phone can be a faster way to reach people, build their excitement, and get their support.

When telephone calls are made asking for a donation on a credit card, the number of paid pledges increases and the average donation goes up, probably because the donor is saved the hassle of mailing a check.

When you send people a letter first, announcing that a phone call will follow, they are usually more receptive and donations usually increase.

b. THE DANGERS OF TELEPHONE FUNDRAISING

Although telephone fundraising may be worth considering, you must beware of certain dangers.

First, telemarketing is not for corporate donations. Avoid telemarketing calls to big businesses when you want a grant. Such calls are not only ineffective, they can be counter-productive. The calls may offend corporate donations officers who prefer the written approach. Worse yet, they may result in small contributions, undermining your ability to get a larger donation from the corporation. Restrict telemarketing to individual donors.

Also, beware of unscrupulous telemarketing shops. Some non-profit organizations have allowed high-pressure telephone canvassers to raise money in their group's name. For example, often the callers may ask people to buy tickets to send disabled kids to the circus or a concert. Many of these telemarketing promoters work on a commission basis, provide all the labor, and guarantee a minimum level of return. This sounds very attractive on the surface, but in reality, it is often costly and damaging for the non-profit. After the telemarketers have deducted their expenses, telephone charges, salaries, and commissions, the non-profit often gets less than 25% of the money raised. Ken's consulting firm worked with one Canadian organization for which a telemarketing firm raised $360,000. The charity only received $60,000.

A study by the Attorney General of Massachusetts showed that the average non-profit ended up with only 29% of the money after telemarketing firms made calls. In nearly one-third of the cases they studied, the return was less than 16%. (For more on this see *The NonProfit Times*, February, 1994, page 12.) State and provincial governments are so upset at these abuses that an increasing number have introduced laws regulating telemarketing.

In fact, costs like these are not out of line compared to other donor acquisition costs. Direct-mail campaigns to acquire new supporters often only break even financially, which means the immediate net proceeds to the non-profit's work is zero.

Another problem with telemarketing shops is that the non-profit often does not get access to the names, addresses, and phone numbers of their new supporters. The telemarketing company may keep these lists.

It took one Canadian charity over a year of legal letters merely to get the carbon copies of the tax receipts with the donors' names. Then the charity had to retype the list onto a computer data base before they could send a second request for funds. A relatively small portion of these expensively acquired new supporters became long-term donors. The delay before the charity could contact them again was just too long.

Commission payments for telemarketing callers are a special problem. The telemarketers often become pushy in order to increase their income. Carefully approved scripts are forgotten as they say whatever they think will produce a donation. The result may be long-term damage to the good name and reputation of the non-profit organization. Donors may give to get rid of the caller, but vow never to support that charity again.

Legitimate telephone canvass firms do not work on a commission basis. This practice is prohibited by the Code of Ethics of the National Society of Fund Raising Executives. If you are approached by commission-based telephone promoters, do not participate.

Legal requirements in many jurisdictions require professionals and even some charities to register before calling donors. This has been introduced to protect the public from fraudulent calls. Check with your lawyer and with the government before you get started.

If you plan to use an outside telemarketing company to make calls, investigate several firms before working out a contract. Look for one that has experience with other non-profit organizations like yours and understands the special attention required. Compare notes on cost, results, their ability to move quickly, and the services offered. Also note the following pointers:

(a) Be wary of companies that claim to have secret lists. These lists are often compiled while the firms conduct campaigns for other non-profit organizations, without the other group's permission. Your donor list could suffer a similar loss of confidentiality.

(b) Talk to the actual telephone operators as well as the firm's salesperson. Decide if the callers can convey your group's message properly. They represent your organization to your donors. Can they answer difficult questions intelligently?

Are the callers recruited from students with a good understanding of your issues, or are they used to selling products like aluminum siding or subscriptions to magazines? Do they sound like they are talking or reading a script? Would you hire them yourself?

(c) Make sure callers are paid a salary, not commission. Commission payments encourage the callers to push too hard. People who are paid a commission know that their pay checks depend on getting the donors to give at once. This ignores the value of the donor's long-term relationship with the organization. Callers have been known to distort information in a manipulative way;

this angers the donors if and when the truth comes out. Paid callers have been known to use abusive language toward people who do not give.

(d) Make sure the script callers use is submitted for your approval and that no changes to the script are allowed without your approval.

(e) Monitor calls periodically to make sure the script is being used as written. Don't hire a firm that won't let you watch. Ask to observe another campaign in progress before you sign a contract.

(f) Make sure you receive all the names and addresses of donors within one month of the campaign conclusion. This must be faster if you are sending the donors a charitable receipt. If you keep your own donor list on a computer, specify that the list be given to you in a computer format that is easy to use and compatible with your existing data base format.

(g) Make sure callers are carefully selected, trained, and rewarded, whether paid or volunteer.

Remember, professional telemarketing is expensive. Staff, telephone lines, rent, long distance, and all the other costs add up rapidly. Many firms will charge an advance start-up fee of several hundred dollars to create the original script and train their callers.

Professional telemarketing costs about four to five times more than sending a letter. In many cases the results are well worth the cost. Only testing will determine for sure.

c. HOW A TELEPHONE CAMPAIGN CAN BENEFIT YOUR ORGANIZATION

If it is done properly, telemarketing can recover lapsed donors because it opens the door to dialogue — provided you have good telephone volunteers. They can probe for the reasons the donors stopped giving and gently woo them back. Knowing why you lost a donor may help you reduce the number of other donors lost.

If they still support your work, but can't give financial aid right now because of their economic circumstances, you may be able to find another way they can support you. Perhaps they would like to volunteer time. Maybe they can give again later. Perhaps a small donation on their credit card of $3 or $5 a month would be easier to give. Perhaps they plan to remember your organization in their will.

You can upgrade current donors. Telephone your middle-level donors. Begin with donors in the $50 plus range. Do not make calls to the very top donors; visit them personally if you can. Also, don't call donors who have given under $50 if you have a shortage of volunteers.

You can also solicit emergency contributions by phone. Many groups exist primarily to cope with emergencies. Examples include the Red Cross, Doctors Without Borders, and St. John Ambulance. For them the telephone is a logical tool.

Even organizations that are not created to handle emergencies might have to act fast if an unexpected situation develops. For example, the furnace might die in the middle of the winter. Pipes might burst. Fires, storms, and natural disasters might affect any group's facilities. In any of these circumstances, an organized telephone campaign can help.

If you are prepared, you can begin making phone calls within hours. Sending letters takes too long.

In a rapidly changing situation, a letter may be out of date by the time it arrives. Telephone scripts can be changed instantly. Prepare for an emergency in advance. The donor's responses might be immediate and generous within a few days of a disaster. Their willingness to contribute might fade fast once the media has moved on to a new story.

During an emergency appeal, organizers must analyze the results of the calls daily to decide when to stop calling.

However, while telephone fundraising can be effective with donors who know your organization, phoning people who have never supported you before is not cost effective. There are a few exceptions to this:

(a) A group has many members or people who have used their services (such as attending a concert or sending kids to a sport), but has never before asked them to give.

(b) A group has names and phone numbers for people who signed a petition for an important cause, and phones to give them a news update and ask for support.

(c) A group is raising money to help in a situation that has received a lot of publicity.

(d) A small-town organization reaches out to neighbors.

(e) A well-known organization approaches people who have heard of it and have similar interests.

Calling people out of the phone book is usually not worth the time, even if the calls are restricted to wealthier neighborhoods, or to executives or professionals listed in directories.

Calls sometimes work with a list of donors rented or borrowed from another non-profit. They might even work with a rented list of subscribers to a magazine, provided the magazine's topic and target audience is narrowly defined to include your supporters. However, such lists may not include phone numbers. As a result, you might have to do extra work or pay extra charges to look up the numbers.

If you want to try recruiting new supporters over the phone, test the process carefully. Compare it to the time and money required to acquire new donors through the mail, through special events, and/or through personal contacts.

Don't solicit your most generous donors on the phone.

d. HOW MUCH COULD YOU RAISE?

Let's assume you start with 100 supporters on your list for whom you have phone numbers. (We won't count those you can't phone.)

Typically, you might actually get through to between 40 and 60 of those. The rest will be out or you will get busy signals.

Of those you reach, 10% to 50% will pledge. The rest will say no. This leaves you with four to thirty people who promised support, out of the original 100.

Of those who pledge, from 50% to 90% will actually send in their contributions. The rest will never get around to it. Now you have from two to twenty-seven real donors.

Average donations will be in the same range as a mail fundraising campaign. For most groups this is from $15 to $35. For a university it might be $500 or more, pledged as $100 a year over five years. For a major health charity, the average gift was $200. For a grass roots group it could be lower. Let's assume at the low end you will actually receive two donations of $15, totaling $30, before expenses. At the high end, you might receive 27 donations of $35, totaling $945 before expenses.

Callers can make about 20 to 25 calls each during an evening session lasting three to four hours. Each call lasts less than five minutes. The average caller completes about ten calls per hour (not counting busy signals and phones that are not answered). The most effective callers talk to fewer people, talk longer, and get bigger donations. Completing these 40 to 60 calls will take from four to six hours.

If you have a volunteer calling, expenses will be low. If you are paying the caller, you will almost certainly lose money at the low end. It is not unusual for professional telemarketers to charge $25 per hour, plus $500 start-up costs. Four to six hours of calls would cost $100 to $150.

These results vary depending on your community, your cause, your callers, your script, and many other variables.

You can lower costs by collecting telephone numbers of all donors ahead of time.

Even if you are not planning a telephone campaign right now, prepare ahead. Finding phone numbers can be time consuming, costly, and frustrating.

e. HOW TO GET DONORS' PHONE NUMBERS

Unless you use the methods below, you may never find the phone numbers for many of your donors. Some have unlisted numbers, some are listed under someone else's name, and some have moved away.

There are several ways to get donors to give you their phone numbers. Use all of these methods. No one technique will succeed in every case.

(a) Request phone numbers on reply coupons used in letters, raffles, events, brochures, and anywhere else you contact donors. Ask the donors directly. Add a line below the space for the donor's name and address on the reply card for the donor's phone number. Most donors will fill this in.

(b) Check their checks. Many people have their phone number printed on their checks. Make sure the people processing donations check for this and collect phone numbers for your data base.

(c) Use a paid service bureau to look up numbers for you, using phone books and/or computerized directories. Some charge for the service, often about 10¢ to 20¢ per phone number. Some do it free for clients who are using other services.

f. HOW TO APPROACH DONORS

Send the letter a week to ten days ahead. In it, tell donors that in a few days they will receive a phone call asking them to give more than they have ever given before. Make this letter long and persuasive. Do not include a reply envelope or reply card — the purpose of the letter is not to get them to give right away, but to set the stage for the phone call.

Sophisticated campaigns will even send two letters. The first, a short note, says "you will receive a letter in a few days." It is from the highest staff person whose name appears at the top of the organization's letterhead. It may include a brochure. The second letter is two to five pages long, from the chairperson of the campaign, on his or her own personal letterhead. It may say the amount the non-profit hopes the donor will pledge.

g. HOW TO CHOOSE AND MANAGE YOUR CALLERS

Should you pay callers or use volunteers? This is not an easy question.

Using volunteers keeps costs lower and can be more effective, because the sincerity in a volunteer's voice cannot be matched by professionals, no matter how well-trained. When staff or paid telemarketers call, the implication is that they are raising money to pay themselves. A call from a volunteer also pleases the donors more, since they feel you are being a good steward of their contributions.

Yet using paid callers also makes sense. You may not be able to get enough volunteers. Your volunteers may not be comfortable raising money on the phone. Paid callers tend to raise more money per hour and experienced callers get significantly better results.

Volunteers will usually only work a few shifts, while paid callers may work for weeks or months, or even years.

You may find it too much trouble to repeatedly train new volunteers.

In either case, choose callers with good telephone manners. Make sure that callers are carefully selected, trained and rewarded. Whether volunteer or paid, good callers often have a connection with the group. Theaters may get actors or performers. Children's groups may get parents to call. A health care group might get patients, nurses, or social workers to call.

Look for callers among people who have sales experience. Receptionists and office workers may also be comfortable talking with people on the phone, while introverts are not.

Paying callers may mean hiring your own team or retaining an outside company. You may wish to hire callers on your own and run the telemarketing operation without using an outside firm. This is particularly easy for organizations like schools that have access to skilled labor. Their inside knowledge of the situation makes them good callers.

Have your callers work two or three evenings a week. A shift should last four hours with no break. Any less than that and they can't keep up their skills. Any more than that and they may burn out.

Borrow an office and keep callers close together. Don't send callers off to phone on their own from their home or work. They may never get around to calling, or they may be interrupted during a call by children or colleagues at work.

Instead, keep the callers in one big room while they make the calls. For a short campaign, you can often borrow an office with many desks and phones close together. This avoids the cost of rent and phone installation.

Ask real estate firms, accountants, lawyers, insurance companies, or any big office. Arrange in advance for keys, security, and payment of any long-distance charges. Ask that their employees clean off their desks that day and put papers away so your callers don't accidentally disrupt work. Clean up afterwards, and leave a low-cost gift and thank-you note for every person who loaned you their desks.

Why keep callers together? The telethon atmosphere keeps callers motivated. Put up progress charts and signs. Set off bells or flashing lights for large donations, or milestones reached. Experienced team members can also stand by to help deal with complicated calls.

Encourage friendly competition among callers. Give prizes to those who get larger contributions, or credit card donations. You may be able to get prizes donated, such as dinner at a local restaurant, a book, or a movie pass.

Start about 5:30 p.m. with training and a light supper. Finish by 9:30 p.m. or 10:00 p.m. Avoid calling on the nights of popular major events, such as sports finals.

Provide callers with the information they need to succeed. Prepare the following information to share with the person making the phone call:

(a) the amount of the donor's last gift,

(b) the date of the last gift,

(c) what motivated the last gift,

(d) any special connections they might have with your group, (such as being a participant in a program), and

(e) any other information you have about who the person is. It would be embarrassing not to know that the donor was a past board member or a former active volunteer.

Provide callers with scripts and train them in what to say and what not to say. Don't let callers decide what to say on their own. While no one should actually read a script word for word, having a set of phrases helps keep the calls short and effective. Some approaches do work better than others. Have the callers do the following:

(a) Smile and say hello and ask to speak to the donor by name.

(b) Give his or her name and the name of the group. (In some areas this is required by law.) If the caller is a volunteer or has a special connection to the group, he or she should say so.

(c) Ask if this is a convenient moment to talk. If not, arrange a time to call back.

(d) Tell the donors why they were selected. It may be because they are past donors, or attended an event. Thank them for their past support.

(e) If you sent a letter ahead, ask if the donors remember receiving it. If so, ask for their reaction. If not, summarize the key points.

(f) Tell them what their donation could do to help people.

(g) Ask for a specific donation. For example, "I see that in the past you gave $50. A number of supporters who gave a similar amount last year have chosen to increase that to $75. Are you comfortable with that?" If they agree, ask them to contribute on their credit card. If they don't want to use credit cards, offer to send a volunteer to pick up the contribution immediately or send a pledge reminder letter the same evening. Put a postage-paid business reply envelope in the pledge letter. Tell the donor on the phone this is coming and ask them to use it.

   If the donor does not agree to a specific donation, callers should ask, "What would you be comfortable giving?" If the donor refuses or has questions, listen and discuss it. If possible, ask again for the gift.

(h) Confirm the donors' addresses and the spelling of their names before you hang up. They may have moved but kept the same phone number. Double check the amount of the gift and any other details.

(i) Say "thank you" whether they give or not. Be polite. Say a friendly good-bye. Keep the relationship warm for next time.

h. FOLLOWING THROUGH ON PLEDGES

Send a pledge reminder letter the same evening the call is made. Give the amount the donor pledged, and an emotional explanation of what the money accomplishes. Add a heartfelt thank you.

Only about half the people who pledge will send back their contribution after this first letter.

If the pledge has not been received in three or four weeks, send a friendly reminder. About 15% to 20% more will respond.

A third reminder will bring in another five to ten percent.

When you call a donor, you may get a busy signal, no answer, another person who says your donor is not available, or an answering machine. (Callers still debate whether or not to leave a message: some consider it polite, others consider the message unproductive time.)

Call back in the next hour, or a few days later. Call back up to three or four times before giving up.

In any case, until you have spoken directly to the donor, the call cannot be considered complete.

About 40% to 60% of your list will not be reached. Send them a letter. This is essential if you have told people in advance that you would call. It is a good idea even if you haven't. You might say "Sorry we missed you when we phoned. Your help is needed to..."

i. DONORS WHO GIVE

Send thank-you letters to all who actually give. These should go out within a day or two of their contribution.

When people say "I'll think about it" it could be a polite brush off, or a serious statement of intent. Thank them for giving appropriate consideration to such an important decision. Provide them with additional information, and offer to talk with them if they have questions.

Many people will not give to a phone appeal unless they receive written information. Others will have specific questions they want answered. Prepare a form letter in advance to simplify responding to them.

j. PEOPLE WHO SAY NO

Thank people even if they turn you down on the phone. Include a bit more information, in case you can still convince them, but don't be a pest. Maybe they will give next time.

Analyze the results of each telephone campaign, and compare them to the results you get with other techniques. For example, you should examine the following:

(a) the average size of donations (usually $15 to $25),

(b) the percentage of calls completed (usually 40% to 60%),

(c) the percentage reached who pledge (usually 10% to 50%),

(d) the percentage of pledges who have paid (usually 50% to 90%),

(e) the number of completed calls per hour (usually about ten per hour),

(f) the percentage of lapsed donors recaptured (usually about 30% to 40%),

(g) the average amount of increase in upgrades,

(h) the cost per dollar raised,

(i) the hidden costs, such as staff time and overhead, and

(j) the number of complaints received compared to the number of donations.

10

HOW TO KEEP THE MONEY COMING

Keep your sponsors informed, keep your promises to sponsors, keep up the quality of your work, keep good fundraising records, keep trying to attract new sponsors, and — with a little luck — you should be able to keep the money coming. It's a simple formula, but a lot of hard work.

a. KEEP YOUR SPONSORS INFORMED

Government sponsors usually require detailed financial accounting, an interim report, and a final report. They will ensure that you report.

Corporate and foundation funders don't make reporting a strict requirement — they just expect it. If they only hear from you when you want money, they won't be impressed.

1. General

If you produce a regular newsletter or magazine for your membership, be sure that you also send it to your sponsors. Send any recent positive press clippings about your group. Press clippings indicate to the sponsor that you are reaching your audience and initiating change.

A one-page professionally printed bulletin should be sent to sponsors quarterly if you can afford it. A news format with catchy headlines and short stories is best. It may not be read in detail, but it will show that you are producing.

Don't forget to send sponsors a copy of your annual report, if you produce one.

2. Projects

Once a project is completed, do a final report that includes an evaluation of the project and a copy of the final product, if there is one. This report should be no more than five pages long. If the final product is a book or slide-show, send it to major contributors only and indicate to other funders that it is available if they wish to see it.

Send the report to all funders who contributed specifically to the project, as well as general contributors who expressed an interest in the particular project. Include a covering letter thanking them for supporting the project and outlining the enclosures. If you have plans to do further work in the same area, indicate this.

Sponsors should be invited to any conference, workshop, or film presentation that they have funded. They probably won't come, but the invitation is a courtesy they will respect. If they do show up, all the better: it helps to build the relationship.

b. RECORD-KEEPING

Failing to keep track of when to approach a particular source can result in missing a funding opportunity. Conscientious donors file funding requests and then make decisions two or four times a year. Most donors, however, make decisions when they feel like it, or close to their fiscal year-end when they can predict the tax benefit of contributions.

Approach funders two or three months before the time when they donated money in the previous year. Make a list of which source donated how much in which month of the previous year. Total the monthly income. Now you know whom to approach in which month during the upcoming year.

This funding approaches schedule will also indicate the slow months and help you plan cash flow. September through November and January through March are usually high-income months. The rest are slow months. Plan your fundraising activities with this information in mind.

To keep your records, you may wish to consider computer software designed specifically for fundraisers. This can cost from a few hundred dollars to many thousand. Ken has a very simple program (available free) for groups with less than 700 donors. Good software is essential for a group that plans to continue fundraising for several years, and grow to have a few thousand supporters or more. If you have more than a few hundred, don't try to save money by keeping records in a word processing program or a data base. The professional fundraising software includes useful systems you might never have considered. It has also been tested by other groups, and frequent upgrades are offered to improve the system further. If something goes wrong, you have an expert a phone call away. However, fundraisers from small, poor groups can get started with good paperwork to keep their records straight.

The three basic paper record-keeping systems are —

(a) approaches in the works log,

(b) donor card file, and

(c) correspondence files.

1. Approaches in the works log

This log puts all the relevant information about your current approaches in one place. It saves checking through your day book to find out when you met with Mr. Blatz, or going through correspondence to find out how much you asked for.

Every fundraiser should have a financial target. If you need to raise $10,000 per month, you can determine how many approaches you must do weekly and monthly to meet that target. You will get discouraged when you're fundraising, and it's easy to procrastinate. From your financial goal, determine the number of letters and meetings per month you need. The log is a constant reminder of whether you're meeting your quota. When it's time to check on the progress of your approach by telephone, the log will indicate who to phone.

Fundraisers should report monthly on fundraising activities to staff or to a member of the board. The log makes that reporting easy.

A format for this log is illustrated in Sample #11.

2. Donor card file

Your donor card file will tell you at a glance how much a donor gave last year, when, and for which project. To set up a file, you need a card file box with 5" x 7" (12 cm x 17 cm) file cards. File them alphabetically by name of funder. Color-coding the cards according to the type of funder — corporate, foundation, or government — can save you some time.

Don't handwrite these cards — type them. You may be able to decipher your own handwriting, but your successor may go crazy trying to read it.

Sample #12 shows an example of a donor card.

3. Correspondence files

Open a letter file for every source you approach. File them alphabetically by name of funder. Keep your filing consistent and up to date. Keep press clippings about funders — mergers, new products, new presidents, donations to other groups — in this file too.

c. MONTHLY DONORS, CREDIT CARDS, AND ELECTRONIC FUNDS TRANSFER

Non-profit groups can raise more money by taking donations on credit cards. They can raise even more with pre-authorized payments and electronic fund transfers. A monthly giving system can be another important source of income.

SAMPLE #11
APPROACHES IN THE WORKS LOG

Funder	Date of letter	Date of phone call	Date of meeting	Amount requested	Date and amt. rec'd	Comments
Blatz Ball-Bearings	Aug. 8	Aug. 15	Aug. 23	$2,000	Nov. 23 $1,500	Water pollution project
Conserver Foundation	Aug. 8	Aug. 15	Aug. 25	$4,000		Natural areas study
Hickle Leasing	Aug. 21	Aug. 29	Sept. 7	$250	Oct. 29 $250	General
Lambten Realty	Aug. 22	Aug. 29	Sept. 12	$500	Nov. 3 NO	Bought out by Master Realty

BLATZ BALL-BEARINGS LIMITED

206 Widget Drive
Cleveland, Ohio
20105

Contact:
Ms. J. Blatz
President
Telephone: 555-4321
Fax: 555-4322

Materials sent:

Oct./94
Annual report

April/95
Water pollution report

Date and amt. req'd	Date and amt. rec'd	Project
Aug./94 $1,000	Oct./94 $1,000	General support
Aug./95 $1,500	Nov./95 $1,200	Water pollution

1. Monthly giving system

About 15% of a charity's donors will sign up for monthly giving plans. This 15% gives a disproportionately high share of their total income.

Monthly plans are increasingly familiar to people through commercial transactions, such as mortgage payments, bank loans, and car payments. Even bills for newspaper subscriptions, phone service, and cablevision can be automatically debited to your account.

Many donors who would not otherwise be able to give generously, can do so on monthly installments. A person might find it hard to give $100 on a single check. The same person might not mind giving $10 a month, even though that totals $120 a year, which is a 20% increase.

Monthly donations provide a reliable cash flow for your organization. This can make your planning easier. The cost to raise a dollar is lower, because the amount given is higher.

It also evens out the income, which is often disproportionately high in the pre-Christmas period, and very low in the summer.

Donors who sign on for monthly giving usually allow the money to be deducted until they request that it stop. This is known as a "negative option" in marketing jargon. It means it is not necessary to convince the donor to give again. This, in turn, reduces the amount of junk mail which might unintentionally alienate some people. Inertia is on your side, since the donor must take conscious action to discontinue giving.

In addition, monthly donors can be sent fewer fundraising letters, thus lowering the cost of communication and wasting less paper. You also send only one single tax receipt at the year end. These savings more than make up for the staff time required to administer the plan and the small fees charged by banks.

While these plans were historically much more popular in Canada than in the United States, they are catching on fast.

2. Credit cards

Donors make larger contributions on credit cards than with checks or cash. Ken's firm has found that gifts are 10% to 25% larger.

Storekeepers and mail-order merchants know that credit card shoppers spend more. Now charities can benefit. Maybe donors give more when they can use their credit cards because it is simpler. For some people, finding their checkbook is hard. Then depression might set in as the donor looks over the bank account balance. Then there is the nuisance of actually writing out a check.

Credit cards are particularly helpful for people who agree to contribute over the phone. Typically younger people are more comfortable with this than seniors.

3. How to get started

Very small groups with only a few donors may find it too difficult to set up their own monthly donor and credit card systems. Perhaps you can find a friendly business person who will let you deposit donations through his or her account. However, donors may become confused when their credit card bill arrives showing a payment to Joe's Pizza instead of your group.

For groups with more than 100 donors, it is probably worth setting up your own system. Here's how.

(a) Encourage donors to write a series of post-dated checks

Post-dated checks are an adequate system of monthly donations, but not as good as credit cards or pre-authorized checking (PAC). People are unlikely to write very many checks at once — seldom more than a year. However, with credit cards and PAC the donations can continue, without further action, until the donor stops them.

In addition, post-dated checks and PAC transfers are occasionally returned by the bank if there are insufficient funds. Credit card donations are almost always honored.

(b) Arrange to accept gifts on credit cards

Contact your bank and ask them to set up a merchant account so you can take donations on both VISA and MasterCard. Groups that deal with upper income people may also wish to add American Express or other credit cards.

Bank fees do apply. Many people are surprised to learn you can negotiate for the best possible credit card fees. Banks usually tell you that you must pay them fees of 5% of the amount deposited. Many charities have arranged fees as low as 1.5%. Negotiations will be easier if you have a board member or friend who is a major customer or employee at the bank, or a respectable community leader, such as a doctor or lawyer.

You also have to open a special clearing account and keep a small minimum balance in the account at all times. Banks may initially insist that you keep a very large amount on deposit to protect themselves against fraud. I have heard of banks expecting non-profits to put up as much as $10,000. Again, this can be negotiated. There will also be a small deposit for the card-impression device. If you are not satisfied with your reception at one bank, ask their competitors.

(c) Make arrangements for automatic monthly deductions from donors' credit cards

Encourage donors to make monthly donations by designing a reply card or pledge form that allows you to deduct a contribution from their credit card each month. This is better than post-dated checks, because the donor does not have to develop a sore arm after the first few checks.

You do not have to have the donor's card to create a deposit slip; this is the same operation that is used in mail-order shopping. Write the donor's card number, expiry date, and name on a credit card slip. In the spot where a signature is required, write S.O.F., which means Signature on File. The credit card company's instruction book will explain all this.

Set up a simple internal reminder system so you can process these donations smoothly every month. Use a 'bring forward' system to note which donors should be charged on each date. Don't be late. If you make your deposit a few days behind schedule, the donor will be irritated to find two payments to you on the same month's credit card statement.

(d) Set the example

Ask the board, volunteers, special friends, and staff to give via the monthly system. This helps cover any minimum volume required to achieve economy of scale.

(e) Ask often

Include monthly giving options in every fundraising appeal to individuals. On a reply form or in a brochure, include a phrase such as the following:

I wish to give   [ ] $5   [ ] $10   [ ] $15   [ ] $20 $_____ to
[name of non-profit group] every month.
Please charge it to my
[ ] VISA   [ ] MasterCard
Card number _____
Expiry date _____ Effective date _____
Name on the card _____
Signature _____

Be sure to leave enough space to fill in the card number, which can be 18 digits long or more.

(f) Expand to pre-authorized checking

Pre-authorized checking (PAC) is also called Electronic Fund Transfer (EFT). This is the same system used by many people to pay installments on car loans, mortgages, and insurance. The bank automatically withdraws the money from the donor's checking account every month and deposits it in the non-profit group's account.

The bank will charge monthly administration fees. These are usually about $35 a month plus 15¢ per donor. It is not cost-effective until you have about 50 donors signed up on monthly donations.

The banks often have complex legal forms they ask people to sign when they register for PAC. These are designed with commercial transactions, such as insurance or car lease payments in mind. Most of the wording is irrelevant to a charity. Fight for the right to use simple, jargon-free wording.

(g) Explore payroll deduction plans

It is increasingly easy for employers to allow employees to have contributions deducted from their paychecks automatically, thanks to new computerized pay systems. However, the hard part is convincing employees to sign on and name your group as the recipient.

Donors can also do this in many areas using payroll deduction plans already set up by the United Way and similar groups. They simply name your group as their designated beneficiary. It may be easier to convince people to do it this way, at first, rather than to set up your own system. The following steps should guide you in preparing your own donor system:

(a) If your non-profit group has employees, begin by setting up a payroll deduction plan for them. You can't ask others to do what you do not do yourself.

(b) Discuss the payroll plan option with the United Way or similar groups in your community. If you receive support from them, be sure you do not endanger an important relationship. Research the methods they use and copy them.

(c) Ask board members to sign up where they work, or if they own or manage companies, to encourage their employees to sign on.

(d) Send letters to your volunteers, clients, and members encouraging them to designate your group on their existing payroll deduction plans.

(e) Approach large employers and ask if you can set up displays or send speakers to address employees.

d. ENCOURAGE ADDITIONAL DONATIONS

Do not send monthly donors all the direct-mail appeals sent to other people, but do write to them at least twice a year. This maintains their awareness and loyalty. It also gives them the option to give an extra amount because of a particular program that appeals to them. A high percentage of monthly donors do this.

Write to them in the pre-Christmas season, when donors are in their most generous mood. For those who do serious tax planning, it is also the last opportunity to give before the end of the calendar year.

Also, write to them in the spring, the second-most generous time of year. Filing tax returns (and in some cases getting tax rebates) may also remind people that they want to give more to charity.

e. UPGRADE DONORS

Contact monthly donors each year to encourage them to increase their gift level. Do this as part of the pre-Christmas appeal.

To summarize, modern forms of payment are gaining popularity among donors and non-profit groups. Monthly donations, credit cards, and electronic fund transfers make it easy for people to be as generous as they want. They also improve cash flow and donor retention. The costs involved are negotiable, and are reasonable for a mid-size to larger group, particularly if you expect the group to be active over several years. Younger donors are more comfortable with this technology, but it is becoming more common everywhere.

11
FUNDRAISING CONSULTANTS

Fundraising consultants are widely used by the larger public interest groups in the United States and are common in Canada. This chapter will tell you when to consider bringing in a consultant, what a fundraising consultant can and can't do for you, and how to get value for your money from a consultant. These suggestions are based on our experience as both staff persons working with consultants and as consultants working with non-profit clients.

a. WHEN TO CONSIDER A CONSULTANT

You should consider bringing in a fundraising consultant when you want to —

(a) try a new method of fundraising,

(b) increase your budget substantially by expanding your funding base,

(c) establish your fundraising on a regular, more predictable, professional basis,

(d) hire your first full-time fundraiser or train your first fundraiser,

(e) deal with a backlog of fundraising materials and reports, or

(f) prepare a fundraising strategy.

b. SELECTING A CONSULTANT

If the above situations sound familiar and you want to investigate using a consultant, here's how to go about it. Contact other fundraisers you know and find out if they have worked with consultants. A recommendation from a fundraiser you trust is a good starting point. If none of your peers has used a consultant, you might try contacting a larger charity or the development office of a nearby hospital or university for suggestions.

The American Association of Fund-Raising Counsel publishes a directory of members. The directory, available free of charge, lists consulting firms, their areas of expertise, and the geographical areas they serve. Both American and Canadian grass roots groups should start by approaching their local chapter of the National Society of Fund Raising Executives, or a similar group locally. To find it, call the professional fundraising staff at a university or hospital; chances are good they will be members. Canadian groups can get a list of consultants from the Canadian Centre for Philanthropy. See the Appendix for addresses of these organizations.

Once you have the names of a few consultants, arrange to meet with each of them. The consultant should not charge you for this initial meeting, but confirm this when you call. Often, fundraisers are afraid to even phone a consultant because they think that the clock will immediately start ticking at $100 to $200 an hour. The first visit is usually free, provided that it is a sales call, and not an attempt to get all your problems solved without paying. Consultants only make a living by selling their time and their ideas. A good consultant can save you untold hours of wasted work, and will give you ideas and systems worth far more than you pay. In our opinion, the consultant is in no position to charge you until you have a signed contract or an agreement. If it doesn't get to that stage, you should be under no obligation. However, the only way to be sure is to ask at the outset.

The initial meeting should be attended by the executive director, the fundraiser, the members of the board who deal with fundraising, and the fundraising consultant. Both the staff and the board should be represented; any experienced consultant will be reluctant to deal with only staff or only board members. Ask the consultant if there is any specific information you should assemble or send to him or her before the meeting.

At the meeting, you assess the consultant and the consultant assesses you. It's a two-way street and both parties will have a lot of questions. You want to find out what the consultant's experience is, who some previous clients are, what specific expertise the consultant has to offer, and what he or she can do for your group. The consultant wants to learn about your programs and activities, your budget and your current donors, and what you expect from him or her. Both parties need to become acquainted and judge whether they will be able to work together.

If you decide to use a consultant, there are several ways to proceed. You could ask the consultant to submit a proposal to you, outlining the work that would be done, how long it would take, and what it would cost. Or you could decide what specific work you want the consultant to do and ask for an estimate on the job. A third option is to agree on an hourly or daily rate and set out the functions the consultant will perform over a specified period of time.

The second option is called a tender or a request for proposal. If you choose this method, do your homework first! Don't send tenders to 28 consultants! That means you are asking 27 consultants to waste their time and in a few weeks you will have to call all 27 and tell them just that. Joyce's policy as a consultant is not to respond to any invitation to tender that was sent to more than five consultants.

The third option is a common billing arrangement, but, if you use it, be sure to make the consultant give you itemized invoices, indicating how much time was spent on individual tasks or functions. You should also inquire about the consultant's billing practices for travel time, expenses for travel and accommodation, evening or weekend meetings, telephone time, and secretarial support.

The larger consulting firms will have many staff people with a range of experience, expertise, and fees. Be sure you are getting the individual you think you are getting. Some firms may send the president or a senior partner out to impress you at the initial meeting, and then send a junior consultant to do the work. You can specify this in the contract by naming the person you want to do the work as the principal consultant.

Some consultants work for a percentage of the money they raise for your group. The advantage to you is that if the fundraising does not succeed, it doesn't cost you any money. This arrangement is controversial. The Code of Ethics of The National Society of Fund Raising Executives specifically prohibits members from working on a commission, for the protection of non-profit groups. Think through how your donors might react. Find out what the consultant plans to do, and be sure *you* retain control.

c. GETTING VALUE FOR YOUR CONSULTING DOLLAR

One of the best ways to get value for your money is to get the consultant to teach you the tricks of the trade and to train you to be a better fundraiser. The one thing the fundraising consultant has and you probably lack is broad fundraising experience. With that professional judgment the consultant can save you a lot of misdirected time and effort. Try to tap that experience and learn as much as you can from the consultant. Make this an explicit part of the contract. Don't have the consultant do work that you can do for yourself or that he or she can teach you to do.

Another cost-effective use of a consultant's time is to have the consultant develop a fundraising strategy and plan for you. The consultant can do the following things:

(a) Provide an objective assessment of your fundraising capability.

(b) Tell you which sectors and which specific sources to approach to fund different projects, how to do it, and who to get to do it.

(c) Interpret the responses to requests and tell you if a new direction or emphasis is indicated.

(d) Determine the fundraising tools and materials you will need for the job.

Researching individual, corporate, and foundation prospects is a task the consultant can do, but it is an ongoing, time-consuming job. It would be better to get the consultant to teach you to do the research yourself.

There are some fundraising functions which, in our opinion, the consultant should not perform. The consultant should not recruit fundraising volunteers or do any face-to-face solicitations for you. He or she can tell you who to recruit, who to solicit, and what kind of rationale to use, but you have to do the person-to-person contact. There are several reasons for this.

If the consultant went door-knocking for you, he or she would end up on the same doorsteps too frequently. In a fundraising meeting, the consultant might have to take a position on an issue, state policy, or make a commitment on behalf of your group. The consultant is not authorized to do this and shouldn't be.

Finally, consultants are concerned about their reputations. They can't be expected to put their reputations behind every client group, especially when they don't have any decision-making power in that group.

d. CONCLUSION

Consultants can play a valuable role in fundraising. The right fundraising consultant at the right time can save an organization a lot of time, effort, and money. Consultants have technique and broad experience, and they should have sound judgment and good instincts. But they don't have any magic sources of money up their sleeves. They know that fundraising is a lot of hard work, and they are prepared to do it for a price. There is no great mystery about it and no reason to be suspicious. Just be sure you have a clear contract, you know each other's expectations, and you say what's on your mind every step of the way.

12
VOLUNTEERS

a. FIGHTING RESISTANCE

One of the few ways to expand your organization's services without increasing payroll is by developing your volunteer capability. However, developing a sound and lasting volunteer program requires care, knowledge, and planning. It may require some effort to even convince your board of directors or your staff to create or expand volunteer activity.

A common reason for resistance to using volunteers is the myth that volunteers, by definition, are not reliable, are not capable, and are not competent. You may hear statements like the following:

"You will spend all this time and energy on volunteers and just when you get them trained, they'll quit."

"You can't trust this important task to a volunteer. It's too critical for the organization."

"You simply can't depend on volunteers."

There is truth in these concerns. In order to counter them, you will need to convince your staff or board that you have a workable plan to deal with these potential problems. Present actual examples of the successful and innovative use of volunteers. Demonstrate to them how the benefits will add up and how you will minimize the costs.

If you decide to proceed, you must educate yourself and your colleagues about working with volunteers. You need to understand what motivates and discourages them. Learn about the volunteer cultivation process, from recruitment and orientation, through training and promotion, and on to retirement.

Is the state of the economy and heavier work commitments destroying volunteerism? Definitely not! Volunteerism has changed since the fifties when stay-at-home mothers seemed to have time available for hours of volunteer work. Now, most volunteers work. Many have university degrees, and the more education they have, the more they volunteer. Women still volunteer slightly more than men, but not much. Volunteers still put in long hours; they are also most likely to be over 35.

b. VOLUNTEER ROLES

Many groups think of volunteers as people who are willing to work endlessly at stuffing envelopes simply out of the goodness of their hearts. There are such people, but this attitude, that all volunteers aspire to nothing more than the low-level jobs no one else wants to do, limits volunteers' potential.

Volunteers now provide direct service in many social service agencies. They may be trained to provide direct service or to work alongside a team of professionals. Previous clients who have benefited from the organization may volunteer to serve new clients. This model is used by Alcoholics Anonymous and Bereaved Families. The individual's personal experience and motivation "to help someone who's going through what I went through," coupled with training in counselling, produce an excellent volunteer.

Many new grass roots social change groups have emerged over the past decade. These groups are often run totally by volunteers who function in many capacities: conducting research, formulating positions and policy, making presentations to government bodies, writing briefs, and issuing press releases. The track record of the volunteers in these groups is impressive, yet volunteers are rarely given these opportunities in traditional charities.

Bringing volunteers into a policy-making or direct service role will have an impact on the professional staff who formerly had exclusive control of those areas. Not only will they have to work with volunteers, but their job may shift from one of direct contact with the client group to that of a trainer and manager of volunteers. The professional may be reluctant to give up the satisfaction of direct contact with the client and may feel threatened or disenfranchised.

To deal with the apprehensions of the staff, involve them in the design of the volunteer development program. Ask the board to draft a policy and set of practices pertaining to the role and function of volunteers. Make a written agreement with your volunteers so that everyone understands and accepts both the opportunities for and the limits to volunteer involvement in decision-making. Identify volunteers who are interested in autonomy and decision-making power, and place them in situations requiring responsibility and initiative.

The volunteer cannot and should not replace paid staff. Volunteers extend and humanize the services, provide a strong and authentic link with the community, inject new energy, imagination, and innovation into the organization. Creative use of volunteer labor should enhance the role of paid staff — not replace it.

c. UNDERSTANDING VOLUNTEERS' MOTIVES

There is a popular assumption that people volunteer out of duty or out of their desire to "do good." While there is some good citizenship in every volunteer, there are as many different reasons for volunteering as there are people. A volunteer's motives are highly personal and you don't need to know all the reasons why each of your volunteers work for you. However, you need to understand and recognize a range of motives so that you can design volunteer jobs to fit the motives.

Most people volunteer because "there's something in it for them." The volunteer job must fill a need. These needs may vary from a need for self-esteem and affiliation, to wanting to help create change or further one's career. Within the business community, taking a position on the board or a committee of a prominent charity is a common method for improving career mobility. It is not for paid staff to judge these motives: you need only ensure that the individual volunteer does not subvert the aims of the organization to further his or her own private interests.

Some people volunteer because they care about a particular issue such as nuclear disarmament, environmental protection, child abuse, or AIDS. Others want to meet new people who hold similar interests and values. Women who work in the home or who are new mothers may volunteer because they need a break from parenting and want contact with other adults. Some people want to be where the action is, and others see volunteer work as an opportunity for personal development. Often people are looking for an outlet which is lacking in other parts of their lives, such as a chance to make decisions or take on a leadership role.

Volunteers give of themselves because they need something. The best way to gain their involvement and commitment is to understand their motives and use that information to place them in a capacity that will meet their needs.

d. FINDING VOLUNTEERS

"Sure, we could use some volunteers around here, but I don't know where to find them," you plead.

Volunteers are all around you. Every person you know and meet is a potential volunteer. The trick is in fitting the volunteer to the job and not being afraid to ask. Personal contacts are a good source of volunteers because by knowing the skills and interests of people, you are in a better position to match them to a job in your agency. The very best way to find volunteers is to ask people you already know.

People who are already volunteers are a likely source because people tend to volunteer for several groups. While this may need to change in the long run, calling on those who are already volunteers will likely be productive. You can find them by seeing who is publicly praised for good volunteer work by other non-profits. Ask other non-profits if they have volunteers they can send your way. Large agencies like hospitals and zoos often have more applicants than they can handle at certain times of year. They may make a referral. Others with cyclical campaigns, such as the United Way, like to keep their volunteers busy in the off-season. You have nothing to lose by asking!

Many medium-sized and large cities have a volunteer bureau and a community information center. Both can help you identify volunteers, and the volunteer bureau may also assist you in training. For example, one mental health center in Ontario offers groups free collating, folding, and envelope-stuffing services, with the labor provided by patients. Critics may consider this exploitation of the patients, but the patients themselves say they are glad to be doing useful work for good causes while developing work skills and relieving boredom. If this practice is not established in your community, you might try approaching various institutions to see if they would be willing to offer such a service.

Retraining centers exist in many communities to help people develop marketable job skills. These may be for women, immigrants, people with disadvantaged backgrounds, or highly skilled people who were laid off when their organization was down-sized. Many retraining centers eagerly seek on-the-job training opportunities for their students. The trainees may be paying for this training, or they may be getting a grant, unemployment insurance, or welfare while they work for you. You may get free help for days, weeks, or months. In extreme cases your group may even get token financial assistance to compensate you for the time you spend with them.

Ask schools if they can help you find volunteers. Colleges and universities often have work-term placements where students gain experience in their chosen career by working with a non-profit group. If you need publicity, ask if a nearby school teaches courses on media relations or journalism. High school, private school, and religious school students in some areas are expected to do volunteer work as part of their curriculum. School placement centers also know that the work experience you can offer looks good on the resume of a student or an unemployed recent graduate. Seniors centers also help match volunteers with groups that need help. You may find people with extensive experience eager to keep busy.

People who recently moved to your community are another good source of volunteers. They are interested in making contacts, and aren't yet over-committed. Ask for help finding them through the Welcome Wagon, the Newcomers Club, schools, places of worship, and real estate agents.

Unelected politicians are another good source. They want to build community profile, and you know a lot about them before you start recruiting. Look at the lists of people who lost recent elections for any level of government from school board to the highest offices and ask them. If all goes well, they'll win the next election and you'll have friends in high places.

Community sentencing programs may also offer you free work, while keeping people out of jail. These programs are for people convicted of minor, nonviolent offences. Some of the people may be unskilled, but able to help you with manual labor. Others may be highly skilled, white-collar people who can help improve your systems. Contact the courts if you think this might fit your group.

Consider asking the people you serve to volunteer. While this is not appropriate in every circumstance, it makes sense for groups involved in arts, sport, social change, adult education, and many kinds of heath care. These volunteers already understand your group. They may bring a unique and helpful view of your work. It may also help build their self-esteem to be part of the helping team, and not only a recipient.

Appeals for volunteers through the mass media may work if your group is well known or if you are working on a high-profile cause. There is also the possibility that the volunteer will contact you directly. Be prepared to deal with volunteers who present themselves.

e. RECRUITMENT AND ORIENTATION

The process of recruiting is often badly neglected. Too often we hear people say, "I went to one meeting and the next time I went they told me I was on the board!" First impressions are hard to change. The recruitment experience establishes the basis of volunteers' expectations. It must be done well.

Before you begin recruiting, clearly establish the need for volunteers, the types of jobs they could perform, and the skills that are required. In other words, what jobs do you have and what kind of volunteers can fill them?

Keep the tasks short at first, unless they require a lot of training or a lengthy commitment. Research shows that almost 80% of people are more willing to volunteer for short-term assignments. Don't assign open-ended tasks, such as handling special events, or joining a committee. Ask them to work on one part of a special event for just two weeks or a month. If you make it rewarding, they may continue on to do more.

Be clear and honest about how much time you expect the volunteer to contribute. Non-profit groups often underestimate the workload, in part because they are afraid of scaring away a badly needed new person by telling the truth. If you tell a volunteer they are needed for less time than they will actually spend, don't be surprised if they only put in what they agreed on, or leave.

Also offer people training. About 70% of people are more willing to volunteer when they receive training.

If your group expects volunteers and board members to make a financial commitment, let them know about this during the recruiting stage. Don't spring it on them later! It is fair to ask volunteers to contribute both time and money, as long as they can make the choice on their own. In fact, people who volunteer give an average of 60% more money than those who do not.

Next, look at your potential volunteers, the people you have identified as prospects, and establish their need, interest, and motivation. Have them complete a form like that in Sample #13. Then you are in a position to find the key: to find the volunteer that best fits the job and the job that best fits the volunteer.

Now you can plan the actual recruitment. The recruitment technique you use should suit your potential volunteers. Will they respond best to a luncheon meeting with you or with a member of the board, or would they be more comfortable at a meeting of friends of the organization? Are they familiar enough with the group to accept an approach from any staff or board person, or would they respond better to an approach from a group member they know personally?

Some people will need to be exposed to the organization before deciding whether to make a commitment. Provide such opportunities regularly through open houses, tours, wine and cheese parties, and other events. If people are interested, give them the chance to see how they like the group and the activity before asking for a commitment. If you push them too soon, you may lose them.

Be sure to use personal follow-up at each stage. Potential volunteers need to feel needed, and to feel that the organization cares about them. The follow-up can be done on the telephone or over coffee. Follow-up is very important in attracting and keeping volunteers.

SAMPLE #13
VOLUNTEER PROFILE

Volunteer Profile

Name:_____

Address:_____

Home phone: _____ Best time to call:_____

Bus. phone: _____ Best time to call:_____

Occupation: _____ Date of birth:_____

Employer/School:_____

1. How many hours per week can you contribute to the program?_____

Please circle days available: M   T   W   TH   F   SA   SU

Commitment for this year:_____

2. Please indicate any previous work experience in other volunteer organizations._____

_____

3. Briefly descibe why you offered to volunteer in this organization (e.g., community involvement, further experience in the field, concern for this cause, etc.).

_____

_____

4. Do you have a specific achievement goal that you plan to accomplish through this volunteer experience?

_____

_____

5. Briefly describe the hobbies and interests that you enjoy.

_____

_____

6. Which of these areas are you interested in? (Check)

[ ] Newsletter committee   [ ] Fundraising
[ ] Advertising   [ ] Develop resources
[ ] Other specific areas _____

Try to find out as much as you can about your prospects' interests, what they think of your cause, what they might enjoy doing with your group. Tell them about the facets of your work and try to get them to identify what they see as their niche in the organization. These recruitment procedures are also part of the orientation process, as the volunteer is becoming familiar with the group, the task at hand, and the people he or she will work with.

Once a prospect agrees to try out a job, provide a period of orientation, a chance to see if he or she likes the position and fits in. Providing the time and the process for new volunteers to check out the organization and their role in it will give you happier and more productive volunteers. Orientation should be matched to the needs of the volunteer. It need not be a long, structured process, but it should make the newcomer feel comfortable and confident in the new setting.

Before volunteers begin working, give them a tour of the office and introduce them to people they will be working with. This is a time for informal chatting, a chance to ask questions and observe work, a chance to break new ground and figure out how they will fit into their jobs. Depending on the nature of the work, you might also want to use group meetings with role-playing sessions to help the new people get used to their new jobs.

Now you can put the volunteers in their new positions and proceed with on-the-job training. But don't abandon them! This is a hard time for them; this is the test. They need a lot of support at this stage and want to feel needed and recognized. Hold regular meetings of new volunteers at which they can share their feelings and experiences in their new jobs. To ensure support and follow-up, you can have supervisors check up on the newcomers and encourage them.

Another approach is to pair new volunteers with more experienced ones. Asking volunteers who have been with you for a number of months to orient new volunteers is often effective. These "old-hands" lend confidence to the newcomers with an attitude that says, "I was just as unfamiliar with this as you are, but soon you will feel as comfortable as I do now." The experienced volunteers can also translate any jargon your organization uses, and introduce the new person to others. The fresh volunteer, in turn, may help re-energize the volunteer who has been around for awhile.

When a volunteer has held a position for several weeks and is prepared to stay, you can ask him or her to write a description of that job and discuss it with you. Make sure that your concept of the job and the volunteer's description of the position match. The more explicit you are about your expectations, the better the chances your volunteer will deliver. You can now ask the volunteer to make a commitment to fill that position for a certain period of time.

If the whole process has gone smoothly, you can let the volunteers begin to work independently. They should now be able to ask for help when they need it.

If a volunteer doesn't like the job after a few weeks but still cares for the organization, see if he or she will try another job. Don't try to keep volunteers in jobs they aren't happy with — if the job doesn't work for the volunteer, the volunteer won't work in the job.

People often complain that it takes a lot of work to get to the point where the volunteer is producing for the organization. It's true! The process of recruitment and orientation *is* labor intensive. If your *only* reason for wanting volunteers is to extend the work of the paid staff or free up the staff for other work, we suggest that you forget volunteers and look into labor-saving devices. It is the combination of the work that volunteers do and their ability to enrich the organization that justifies the investment for both parties.

f. TRAINING, PROMOTION, AND APPRECIATION

Once new volunteers are working well, you must still provide periodic training and growth opportunities. Volunteers need renewal, stimulus, feedback, and change, or they become stale and lose interest. A combination of formal and informal training will fill this need for several years. Training can range from simply passing on an interesting magazine article to sending volunteers to seminars and conferences. Many continuing education programs offer courses that are good training for volunteers. The costs of training should be borne by the organization.

Give your volunteers regular opportunities for reflection and self-evaluation. This way, both you and the volunteer can identify when he or she is ready for a change or a promotion. If you promote a volunteer within the organization, he or she will again need to go through orientation and training stages. Don't drop an old volunteer into a new job without support.

Sometimes, a volunteer's growth may require that he or she move to another agency. What is most important is that the voluntary community as a whole can continue to provide new and exciting opportunities for the volunteer and benefit from his or her efforts. Keep volunteers' best interests in mind and be aware of their changing needs. That is the organization's side of the contract with the volunteer. Besides, if you fail to meet their needs, you will soon lose them anyway.

If several groups can cooperate and pool their efforts in identifying, recruiting, and training volunteers, everybody stands to gain. The chances of gaining new volunteers and promoting others will be far greater through interagency cooperation. Some areas have "volunteer centers" which match up volunteers and agencies.

Providing thanks and recognition to your volunteers should be a regular feature of the program — not something that is only done when the person leaves. It may be as informal as a birthday or Christmas card, or as formal as a presentation of a plaque at a banquet. Do it in a manner that is appropriate for the individual. The thanks will carry more meaning if it is personalized.

g. RETIREMENT AND SUCCESSION

Too many groups try to hang on to their volunteers, begging them to stay on, making them feel guilty for leaving. This is most unfortunate because the volunteer leaves the organization with a bad taste in the mouth, and that doesn't serve the individual or the group. Let your volunteers retire gracefully, with thanks and recognition. When they want to quit, accept it and thank them.

If the person's leaving creates a great gap, it may be appropriate to ask the retiring volunteer to recruit another person to fill the job. Of course, in the best of all worlds you would have a successor waiting in the wings to replace a key volunteer who retires. This is called succession planning. Sample #14 can be used to develop and evaluate possible successors for a key job and plan the recruitment. In many cases, you can get retiring volunteers to train their own replacements. It's efficient, effective, and everybody feels good.

In some groups, the volunteer jobs switch over at an annual meeting. Joyce's own alumni association works that way. Since members and volunteers are spread across the country, succession planning is essential. Joyce has developed a simple form to help retiring volunteers explain their jobs to new volunteers (see Sample #15).

h. THE VOLUNTEER AS FUNDRAISER

"Why is fundraising different from any other volunteer job?" Almost nobody wants to do it and just about everybody is afraid to do it. In fundraising, failure is visible and public. As a result, there are more ways to avoid fundraising than any other job, with the possible exception of defrosting the freezer!

The resistance to fundraising is incredibly high. Your fundraising volunteers will need a lot of work. They need support, encouragement, and training. If your volunteers are doing telemarketing, canvassing, or face-to-face fundraising, they need to be trained specifically for those techniques. The learning curve is all at the front end. Once they are trained and they succeed, they will keep producing for you.

One of the most positive and exciting fundraising committees we have ever seen was headed by a vice president of sales from Xerox. He ran the fundraising like a sales campaign. The committee loved it. If your fundraising committee is dragging its heels, recruit a top sales person.

There have been times when, after the training session and everything else, board members have said, "There's no way I can do this. I can't ask for money." You could say "Sure you can!" and invalidate their concern. Instead, say "I understand. Is there another way you could help us with raising money?" Your volunteers have to be comfortable with their participation in fundraising or they won't succeed.

i. MANAGING STAFF/VOLUNTEER RELATIONSHIPS

If surveyed, probably 40% of volunteers would report that they had been abused in their volunteer position and another 40% would report themselves dissatisfied with how they are managed. Only 20% would say that they are pleased with the way they are treated by the organizations they serve. What qualifies as volunteer abuse? Consider this short list of examples:

(a) Placing Jane Novice, a first-time volunteer, on the board committee that faces the most controversial issues. After the unsuspecting Jane has accepted, you tell her that these issues exist, the chair has just resigned, she is currently a committee of one, and she will have to recruit the rest of the committee members.

SAMPLE #14
SUCCESSION PLANNING SHEET

POSITION TO BE FILLED			BY WHEN	
Potential candidates	Candidate's interests	Rank candidates	Possible recruiters	Possible contacts

Steering Committee Position Description

Position title: _____

Position previously filled by: _____

Telephone number: _____

Major activities:

_____

_____

_____

_____

_____

Major responsibilities:

_____

_____

_____

_____

_____

Reports to:

_____

_____

Average time/month required:

_____

_____

Materials, resources, or access: (e.g., printing, computer time, etc.)

_____

_____

_____

(b) Plunging Jane into demanding action such as counselling or handling a crisis phone line alone with no orientation, training, or back-up support.

(c) Keeping Joe Faithful, a longtime volunteer, stuck in the same job year after year, long past the time when he is bored and wants to progress to new challenges and responsibilities.

(d) Allowing John Oldtimer, one of the original board members, to continue wasting his time and talents on an organization that doesn't want what he is offering.

   "Oh, that's John Oldtimer. He's been on the board forever. He comes to every meeting and talks and talks and nobody listens. We all just wish he'd quit, but he never will." So old John is patronized and insulted because nobody has the decency or courage to ask him to resign. Try to put yourself in old John's shoes.

(e) Asking Kim Peaceful to take on more responsibility or give a speech as a "reward" for good work, when Kim just wants to be allowed to continue doing familiar, relaxing tasks within her competency.

That's a mere start to the list of abuses that staff members perpetrate against volunteers and volunteers sometimes perpetrate against each other. Now, let's take a look at the other list — the volunteers staff members hate.

(a) Alice Professional, who demands that the underfinanced community group that she has deemed worthy of her time measure up to her professional standards.

(b) Alex Runsitall, the committee member who wants to have a say on all important matters, even though his committee meets only once a year.

(c) Annie Condescension, who treats volunteer work like a third rate proposition. She is frequently heard to say, "It's only volunteer work — it doesn't have to be perfect — they won't mind if it's late..." This attitude does more to create staff disrespect of volunteers than anything else — except no delivery at all!

(d) Alan Overrule, who ignores professional staff judgments. Often found on boards or committees, he works hard to make decisions on matters that he is not qualified to judge. We once heard about a Mr. Overrule who, as a newly recruited board member, ordered removal of a structure that was basic to the group's treatment methodology. His action resulted in mayhem within the facility.

Given the experience of both volunteers and staff with these kinds of abuse, it's no wonder that concern about volunteers continues to appear on the priority lists of conferences. But what are the solutions?

"Maybe we need to put more effort into recruitment," said a client of ours who was worried about volunteer turnover. "You had better find out why they are leaving in the first place," we suggested, "otherwise you will just lose them as fast as you recruit them."

Volunteer turnover, poor attendance at meetings, low morale, low productivity — there are no simple equations that will diagnose the cause and prescribe the cure. The same symptom, such as volunteer turnover, could have five different causes in five organizations, and five different solutions, as well.

The first step in finding the solution in your organization is for senior staff and volunteers to admit that there is a problem. This is critical, because if they don't recognize the problem, they won't see the need for a solution. Then determine whether the people involved are truly willing to work to change the status quo. Don't assume that recognition of the problem means a commitment to change. Most people hate change.

If you can negotiate these two steps successfully, you are in a good position to analyze the situation. Start interviewing volunteers and staff to find out how they see each other, what they've experienced, and what they think the problems and solutions might be. Using this information, take a look at the big picture. What are the key issues? Is it leadership? Is it structure? Is it relationships between staff and volunteers or between different levels of volunteers?

When you have a comprehensive analysis in hand, you will know where changes need to be made to improve your organization. Enlist the help of those who were ready to recognize the problems and seem willing to change things to solve those problems.

j. CONCLUSION

This approach to volunteer management is a lot of work, but it's an approach that's based on the realities of running an organization. More important, it works. Whether you can develop your organization to its fullest potential depends on expanding your people resources when your dollar resources are fixed or shrinking. To meet the growing demands from your constituencies, you must be positive, forward-looking, and innovative.

13
STRATEGIES FOR SURVIVAL

a. BE SELF-SUFFICIENT

The best survival strategy for non-profit organizations is self-sufficiency. Public interest groups should make a deliberate attempt to function as a self-sufficient, non-profit business. Many non-profit groups give away potentially marketable products. If there is a need for what you are doing — be it a book, newsletter, or film — in many cases you should be able to sell it and break even financially.

The voluntary sector needs an injection of marketing and entrepreneurial skills. It needs people who can interest a target public in a cause, and convince them to invest their money in it.

b. BUILD UP YOUR ORGANIZATION

Building an organization as the vehicle to carry forward your mission is a survival strategy. That may sound like a blinding glimpse of the obvious, but there are a lot of neglected organizations out there. The volunteers, staff, resources, structures, policies — all the things which, together, make up an organization — cannot be taken for granted. The care and feeding of the organization is a necessity, not a luxury. If you don't take care of your organization, your organization will not be able to shoulder the burdens you want it to carry and your cause will be short-lived.

Within your organization, strive to build a strong, committed staff and board. When it comes to the crunch, when a group is on the brink of bankruptcy or oblivion, only a strong staff and board can pull it together and save it from falling apart.

c. ENCOURAGE DIVERSITY

Developing diversity within the organization will help ensure its survival. Diversity means having a racial, social, economic, and cultural mix within your board of directors. It means listening to your critics and lunching with your perceived enemies. Encouraging diversity means getting all the actors, all the people who have a stake in the issue, to sit down together. It means getting clients working as staff or board members to keep you honest and make sure you don't get pushed off your mission.

Diversity means listening to your funders and recruiting them as volunteers and consultants. Rosabeth Moss Kanter, a well-known management consultant, was asked, "What makes a good consultant?" She replied, "You have to be able to go into an organization you know nothing about, walk around in it for an hour, and say something intelligent about it." Consultants can do that because they are *outside* the organization. So listen to outsiders, they can tell you things about your group that you cannot see for yourself.

Diversity within your leadership gives you an early warning system for outside change that could affect you. If you are involved with social and political issues, your organization is very vulnerable to changes in legislation, in political agendas, and in funding priorities. If you have a diverse board, you have more radars to warn you so that you can adjust in time. Diversity gives you adaptive capacity. Without it, your group could go the way of the dinosaur.

d. MANAGE CONFLICT

Diversity *is* important and powerful for organizations, but many groups are afraid of it, knowing intuitively that the price of diversity is conflict. Most people think conflict is bad and should be avoided, but conflict in organizations is inevitable, necessary, and healthy if you learn to manage it properly. It's only bad if you avoid working it through or if you personalize it.

Entire books have been written on conflict, and this isn't one of them. When you sense conflict between individuals, groups, or departments, get on it fast. Fed by avoidance, conflict will grow and it can become debilitating. Don't hesitate to get outside help if you need it.

Some of the most exciting and high-performing teams we have worked with were those that could manage conflict. Team members would openly state and explain different points of view and the group would work on the differences. The goal of the discussion wasn't to be right or to win, it was to look at all the information, ideas, and implications and work through them to a consensus. The energy that comes from this kind of conflict resolution and the efficacy of the decision-making can carry a team a long way.

e. ENSURE QUALITY

The most common mistake made by non-profit groups is trying to do too much with too little, too fast. They have undisciplined passion and short-sighted strategies. Trying to change the world overnight achieves high staff and volunteer burnout, crisis fundraising, low credibility in the constituencies you are trying to influence, and an early demise. The quality of the group's work deteriorates.

Whether your group runs a program, provides a service, produces a booklet, or does research, focusing on quality instead of quantity will keep you on the right track. Use the quality of the work you do as a check against the seduction of undisciplined passion. A group that limits its mandate and ensures that what it does, it does well, has a good strategy for survival.

f. CONTINUE LEARNING

Let your organization be about learning and having fun. Children learn through play and so do adults. People who are given the opportunity to learn and grow in their work are the most productive.

Be theory-based in your work. Determine which theories work or don't work for you, but don't assume you know better than all the research and all the theorists. That is simply arrogance. Kurt Lewin, one of the founders of organization development, said, "There is nothing so practical as a good theory." Make the theories work for you.

g. CONCLUSION

There is an incredible range of non-profit groups in North America who are working to build a better society by helping abused children, former psychiatric patients, First Nations people, illiterate people, people with illnesses, immigrants, or minority language groups; by saving historical buildings, the environment, animals, or dead elm trees; or by addressing any of the countless other causes that are part of our world.

We hope we've given you a few shortcuts to financing social change.

AFTERWORD

What follows was written by Joyce's dear friend and mentor, the late Dick Arima, a top management and organization development consultant of international repute. For those of us in helping organizations and helping roles, this goes to the heart of the challenges and dilemmas we face.

FAIRNESS

For those who want to help the less privileged — whether they are disadvantaged by gender, race, social status, age, or another reason — the question of fairness becomes an issue at one time or another. How can the less privileged get a fair chance in institutions and organizations? Recent revisions in the Canadian Human Rights Act address this question.

All organizations have rules governing employment, membership, promotions, terminations, and hierarchies within the group. While some of these rules are explicit and formalized, others are implicit and subjective. Hence, extending fair play privileges to the less privileged entails not only attention to the formal rules, which are relatively easy to monitor, but to the informal rules as well. These informal rules present difficulties because the perpetrators themselves are often not conscious about them.

If you want to help the less privileged, you should understand your personal stand on fair play. If you do so, your aid will be more consistent and focused. You will also avoid ambivalence on the issue, an ambivalence which is likely to be detected by those you are helping.

Use the list below to help you identify your attitude toward how society should deal with inequality.

(a) Patronization: Maintain the rules and systems of the privileged, reward the less privileged who work hard and "know their place in life."

The helper who espouses this value teaches the less privileged how to be effectively compliant and how to stay out of trouble. The consequence for the less privileged is that it will help them to survive. However, they will remain subjugated.

(b) Competition: "Every man for himself." Democracy is based on individual hard work and aspiration and the cream will rise to the top regardless of the system.

The helper who espouses this value enables individuals to become more competent and competitive. The consequence for the less privileged is that individuals may gain some of society's rewards such as better pay, jobs, or housing. However, these individuals will have to be overachievers in order to compete with the privileged and could be disappointed if there are ceilings for such rewards for the less privileged.

(c) Assimilation: don't fight the rules — adapt to them. Work harder and work smarter.

The helper who espouses this value ensures that the less privileged understand the rules. Additionally, the helper can enable the less privileged to work effectively within the bounds of the rules.

The consequence for the less privileged is that the rewards will be more bountiful than competition without awareness of the rules. However, through assimilation people can lose their sense of cultural identity and in hard times all the effort that went into assimilating does not guarantee continued privileges.

(d) Compensation: extra assistance to the less privileged because they are starting off with a handicap. They are not the inventors of the rules nor the maintainers and, therefore, they start at a point behind the privileged.

The helper who espouses this value advocates the cause of the less privileged — sponsoring and championing them and challenging the formal and informal rules on their behalf. It is expected that the less privileged will work to help themselves during this advocacy.

The consequence for the less privileged is more equality of privileges because organizations become more aware of unfair rules. However, overdependence on sponsors may lead to feelings of inadequacy.

(e) Equality: strive for pluralism, an integration of diverse cultural characteristics in organizations rather than one culture group dominant over other culture groups.

The helper who espouses this value assists the less privileged to value their cultural heritage. The helper can do what is possible to assist institutions to value other culture contributions and to change those systems that deny those contributions.

The consequence for the less privileged is equal opportunity, not only in employment, promotions, and other concrete rewards, but also in formulating the formal and informal rules by which these benefits are awarded.

Dick Arima
1986

APPENDIX

Here is a partial list of resources you may find useful. There are many others. A listing here is not an endorsement. Being left out is not condemnation. Please contact Ken Wyman if your favorite is missing.

Contact the organizations listed for prices and current information. They may charge extra if your payment does not accompany the order.

a. ORGANIZATIONS

American Association of Fund Raising Counsel
25 West 43rd Street
New York, NY 10036
Tel: (212) 354-5799
Fax: (212) 768-1795

Association of Vancouver Island Fund Raisers (AVIFR)
P.O. Box 45004
Mayfair P.O.
Victoria, BC V8Z 7G9

B.C. Association of Fundraising Professionals
1155 West Pender Street, Suite 708
Vancouver, BC   V6E 2P4
Tel: (604) 682-7447

Canadian Centre for Philanthropy (CCP)
1329 Bay Street, Suite 200
Toronto, ON M5R 2C4
Tel: (416) 515-0764
Fax: (416) 515-0773

CCP covers all aspects of organizational management as well as fundraising. Their extensive Toronto reference library with over 1,500 volumes is open to the public. Special seminars on a variety of topics. Monthly newsletter. Offers computerized foundation searches. Membership fees and charges apply to services.

CCP Publishes *The Canadian Directory to Foundations*, which gives details of available funding, cross-indexed by subject, geography, and individual names. The directory outlines the criteria and interests of every Canadian foundation and many American foundations that give to Canadian charities, including the name and address of the contact person. The directory also shows how much was given, to which charity, and for what purpose. There are also excellent articles on how to get foundation grants. Read these before submitting any applications.

The Centre also publishes a companion guide, *Building Foundation Partnerships: The Basics of Foundation Fundraising and Proposal Writing* by Ingrid van Rotterdam. The guide covers everything you need to know to locate and attract foundation funding, including critical first steps, the ABCs of research, and the essentials of a successful program plan and proposal.

CCP's list of publications also includes *Planning Successful Fund Raising Programs*, by Ken Wyman. How and when to plan, who to involve, how to find time. Includes homework exercises and checklists that you can use to improve your planning process now.

Canadian Society of Fund Raising Executives
Dree Thomson, President
c/o Activations
614 - 22nd Avenue, SW
Calgary, AB T2S 0H8
Tel: (403) 229-9766
Fax: (403) 229-9146

Membership group. Members and chapters in several cities across Canada. Seminars, training, code of ethics, and monthly lunches.

Independent Sector
1828 L Street NW
Washington, DC 20036
Tel: (202) 223-8100
Fax: (202) 223-0609

A non-profit coalition of over 800 corporate, foundation, and volunteer members created as an information exchange and spokes-group. Publishes variety of books, pamphlets. Membership dues based on size of organization (0.25% of salaries paid), but no cost to be added to mailing list for publications catalogues and updates.

National Society of Fund Raising Executives
1101 King Street, Suite 700
Alexandria, VA 22314
Tel: (703) 684-0410 or (800) 666-FUND
Fax: (703) 684-0540

National Society of Fund Raising Executives
(Greater Toronto Chapter)
Bill Hallett, President
YMCA of Metropolitan Toronto
15 Breadalbane Street
Toronto, ON M4Y 2V5
Tel: (416) 324-4123

Membership group for professionals. Monthly lunches. Good newsletter. Holds major conference. American group publishes a journal.

Ottawa Fund Raising Executives
c/o Josephine Uguccioni
York Mailings
309 - 1228 Old Innes Road
Ottawa, ON K1B 3V3
Tel: (613) 745-2171

A group of professionals whose main function is fundraising. The primary purpose is professional development and networking opportunities for individuals.

Ottawa Fund Raisers' Network
c/o Mr. Mahonri Young
366 Daly Street
Ottawa, ON K1N 6G9
Tel: (613) 789-5714

The Network brings together fundraisers in the national capital area to exchange ideas and experiences for mutual benefit. Participates in courses at Algonquin College.

Resource Centre for Voluntary Organizations (RCVO)
Grant MacEwan Community College
Room C132
10070, 104 Street
Edmonton, AB T5J 4S2
Tel: (403) 441-4623
Fax: (403) 441-4663

Free, self-help resource library, including demo disks of computer fundraising programs. Also provides educational material, free speakers, newsletter, audio visual materials, referrals, free boardroom for meetings. Focus is on fundraising, marketing, volunteer and organizational management, and board development.

b. PUBLICATIONS AND CORPORATE DONATIONS

Canadian Business
Canadian Business 500
CB Media
70 The Esplanade, 2nd Floor
Toronto, ON M5E 1R2
Tel: (416) 364-4266

Magazine about Canadian business, with annual listings of the biggest.

The Canadian Centre for Business and the Community
The Conference Board of Canada
Ottawa:
255 Smyth Road
Ottawa, ON K1H 8M7
Tel: (613) 526-3280
Fax: (613) 526-4857

Toronto:
55 University Avenue, Suite 1800
Toronto, ON M5J 2H7
Tel: (416) 360-2372
Fax: (416) 360-2905

Calgary:
714 - 1st Street SE, 3rd Floor
Calgary, AB T2G 2G8
Tel: (403) 233-0720
Fax: (403) 262-3436

The Centre is a non-profit organization affiliated with The Conference Board of Canada. It provides objective information and analysis in the area of corporate giving. It is set up to serve corporate donors, not charities. However, it does have a variety of interesting publications for sale. We have quoted liberally from their work throughout.

The Centre recommends that any group launching a corporate donations request send information about themselves to the Centre's *nearest* office (*not* to all of them). While the Centre cannot match non-profit groups with donors, it wants to have background data handy in case the companies ask for information.

The Ten Lost Commandments of Fund Raising
The Council for Business and the Arts in Canada
P.O. Box 7, Suite 1507
401 Bay Street
Toronto, ON M5H 2Y4
Tel: (416) 869-3016
Fax: (416) 869-0435

The CBAC is an organization of businesses whose purpose is to encourage corporate support for the arts through research, seminars, publications, counselling, and information services. CBAC offers a long list of excellent publications. They do not give money, but can provide limited help to arts groups that need to connect with corporate supporters.

The Directory of Corporate Giving in Canada
Rainforest Publications Inc.
404 - 2010 Barclay Street
Vancouver, BC V6G 1L5
Tel: (604) 684-7729 and (800) 655-7729

This two-volume set profiles the largest corporations in Canada. There is nothing else like it. Unfortunately, because of the rapidly changing nature of the corporate world, this directory is inevitably incomplete and often inaccurate despite the best efforts of the editors. Double-check names and addresses before using them. Extremely expensive.

Canadian Key Business Directory
Dun and Bradstreet
365 Bloor Street East
Toronto, ON M4W 3L4
Tel: (416) 963-6500

Data on corporations. Rapid corporate mergers and personnel changes mean you must do final double-check on names and addresses by phone.

Scott's Directories
Southam Information and Technology Group
1450 Don Mills Road
Don Mills, ON M3B 2X7
Tel: (800) 668-2374 or (416) 442-2070
Fax: (416) 510-6875

Directories of businesses. Volumes on the manufacturing sector for Ontario, Quebec, Western Canada, and Atlantic Canada. *The Toronto Business Directory* covers Metro Toronto only and includes a wider range of businesses, totaling 22,000 listings, organized alphabetically,

233

by street, and by type of product. Listings of the key executives, number of employees, etc.

c. DIRECT MAIL

The Canadian Direct Marketing Association
1 Concorde Gate, Suite 607
Don Mills, ON M3C 3N6
Tel: (416) 391-2362

Over 700 members include business and government. Fundraisers and telemarketers have special groups. Chapters in Montreal, Calgary, Ottawa, and Vancouver, and forming elsewhere. Various fees. Useful information and books (some free) on direct marketing. Seminars and conventions across Canada. Awards for best mailings.

Direct Mail Fund Raising
Public Management Institute
358 Brannan Street
San Francisco, CA 94107
Tel: (415) 896-1900

One of the finest tools. Full of helpful charts and sheets to check off each stage as you go. They also publish a variety of other books. Ask for the catalogue.

Fund Raising Letters
Jerry Huntsinger
Emerson Publishers
Box 15274
Richmond, VA 23227
Tel: (804) 266-2499

A substantial binder full of materials from one of the most experienced direct mail copywriters in the U.S.A.

d. FOUNDATIONS

Canadian Directory to Foundations, 11th edition
Rose van Rotterdam
Canadian Centre for Philanthropy
1329 Bay Street, 2nd Floor
Toronto, ON M5R 2C4
Tel: (416) 515-0764
Fax: (416) 515-0773

Council on Foundations
1828 L Street NW
Suite 300
Washington, DC 20036
Tel: (202) 466-6512

Foundation Center
79 Fifth Avenue — 2nd Floor
New York, NY 10003-3076
Tel: (212) 620-4230 or in the U.S. (800) 424-9836
Fax: (212) 807-3677

Publishes a wide variety of books on foundations and related fundraising. Guides to foundations for 30 different fields. Free catalogue.

The International Foundation Directory 1994 (6th Edition)
Gale Research Company
Penobscot Building
Detroit, MI 48226
Tel: (313) 961-2242

This directory of international foundations, trusts, and other similar non-profit institutions provides a comprehensive picture of foundation activity on a world scale.

Private Foundations Directory
Rainforest Publications
404 - 2010 Barclay Street
Vancouver, BC V6G 1L5
Tel: (604) 684-7729
Tel: (800) 655-7729

Private Foundations Directory lists 3,000 private foundations in Canada in six volumes by area of interest: health care, social services, education, arts and culture, religion, and miscellaneous.

e. FUNDRAISING OVERVIEW

Advancing Philanthropy
Publications Department
National Society of Fund Raising Executives (NSFRE)
1101 King Street, Suite 700
Alexandria, VA 22314-2967

Official journal of the NSFRE. Information, issues, and answers on philanthropic development. Included with NSFRE membership.

Fund Raising For Stability: Strategies for Community Fund Raising
Robert Doyle and Catharine de Leeuw
Social Planning Council of Metropolitan Toronto
2 Carlton Street, Suite #1
Toronto, ON M5B 1J3
Tel: (416) 551-0095

Good book on general fundraising. Understands the community perspective. Includes principles, planning, sources of support, preparing a proposal, innovations.

The Grass Roots Fundraising Book:
How to Raise Money in Your Community
Joan Flanagan
Contemporary Books
180 North Stetson Avenue
Chicago, IL 60601
Tel: (800) 621-1918 or (312) 540-4500
Fax: (800) 998-3103 or (312) 540-4687

In Canada:
Fitzhenry & Whiteside
195 Allstate Parkway
Markham, ON L3R 4T8
Tel: (800) 387-9776 or (905) 477-9700
Fax: (905) 477-9179

Organizing Special Events and Conferences
Darcy Devney
Pineapple Press, 1989
P.O. Drawer 16008
Sarasota, FL 34239
Tel: (819) 952-1085

A practical guide for busy people.

Successful Fundraising: A Complete Handbook for Volunteers and
Professionals
Joan Flanagan
Contemporary Books
180 North Stetson Avenue
Chicago, IL 60601
Tel: (800) 621-1918 or (312) 540-4500
Fax: (800) 998-3103 or (312) 540-4687

In Canada:
Fitzhenry & Whiteside
195 Allstate Parkway
Markham, ON L3R 4T8
Tel: (800) 387-9776 or (905) 477-9700
Fax: (905) 477-9179

Voluntary Action
Canadian Identity Directorate
Department of Canadian Heritage
Ottawa, ON K1A 0M5
Fax: (819) 953-4131

They produce a wide variety of free materials for Canadian non-profit organizations, including four books by Ken Wyman. Quantities are limited to two per organization. Ask for an up-to-date list of all publications available.

f. HOW TO START AND RUN A NON-PROFIT ORGANIZATION

Achieving Excellence in Fund Raising
Henry A. Rosso and Associates
Jossey-Bass Inc.
350 Sansome Street
San Francisco, CA 94104
Tel: (415) 433-1740
Fax: (415 433-0499

A detailed guide written under the direction of one of America's most distinguished fundraising professionals. Winner of the 1992 NSFRE Research Prize.

Fighting for Hope: Organizing to Realize Our Dreams
J.N. Kuyek
Black Rose Books
#888 - 3981 Boulevard St. Laurent
Montreal, PQ H2W 1Y5
Tel: (514) 844-4076

Practical ideas on community organizing, forming groups, holding meetings, planning, funding, and community economic development.

Forming and Managing a Non-Profit Organization in Canada
Flora MacLeod
Self-Counsel Press
1481 Charlotte Road
North Vancouver, BC V7J 1H1
Tel: (604) 986-3366

Managing the Nonprofit Organization
Peter F. Drucker
Harper-Collins, 1990
1995 Markham Road
Scarborough, ON M1B 5M8
Tel: (416) 321-2241

Money, Money, Money — How to Get It!
T. Ouellette
Alberta Council On Aging
501-10506 Jasper Avenue
Edmonton, AB T5J 2W9

How to incorporate and register as a charity, market your project, write proposals for government and foundations, plan special events, and more.

g. IN KIND DONATIONS

In Kind Canada
John Page, Executive Director
7003 Cadiz Crescent
Mississauga, ON L5N 1Y3
Tel: (905) 567-9919
Fax: (905) 826-0272

Gifts In Kind America
700 North Fairfax Street
Alexandria, VA 22314
Tel: (703) 836-2121

The National Association for the Exchange
of Industrial Resources (NAEIR)
Gary C. Smith, President
560 McClure Street
Gailsburg, IL 61401
Tel: (309) 343-0704

h. WHERE TO GET MONEY: OTHER DIRECTORIES

Directory of Employee Charitable Trusts
Rainforest Publications
404 - 2010 Barclay Street
Vancouver, BC V6G 1L5
Tel: (604) 684-7729
Tel: (800) 655-7729

The Directory of Employee Charitable Trusts covers 580 often undiscovered employee operated trusts in Canada.

Handbook of Grants and Subsidies:
Government Aid to Nonprofit Organizations
Canadian Research and Publications Centre (CRPC)
33 Racine Street
Farnham, PQ J2N 3A3
Tel: (800) 363-1400

KWIC Index to Your Ontario Government Services
Ontario Government Bookstore
880 Bay Street
Toronto, ON M7A 1N8
Tel: (416) 326-5300 or
Tel: (800) 268-7540

One route to Ontario grants. Frustrating, but nothing better available.

i. GOVERNMENT REGULATIONS: CANADA

Canadian Taxation of Charities and Donations
Arthur B.C. Drache, Q.C.
CARSWELL
Thompson Professional Publishing
One Corporate Plaza
2075 Kennedy Road
Scarborough, ON M1T 3V4
Tel: (416) 609-3800 or (800) 387-5164
Fax: (416) 298-5094

Expensive, but your lawyer and accountant should review it on any difficult matters. Updated as new regulations are released.

Revenue Canada
Charity Law Hotline
(800) 267-2384

Internal Revenue Service
Exempt Organizations Information
(800) TAX-1040

Official answers for charities, non-profits, and donors on their regulations. You can call anonymously. Free.

Securing Your Organization's Future
Michael Seltzer
The Foundation Center
79 Fifth Avenue - 2nd Floor
New York, NY 10003-3076
Tel: (212) 620-4230 or (800) 424-9836
Fax: (212) 807-3677

j. MAJOR GIFTS AND PLANNED GIFTS

Canadian Association of Gift Planners
Box 1091, Station F
Toronto, ON M4Y 2T7

Canada's first professional body dedicated solely to the development and growth of gift planning. Their work may be too complex for most grass roots groups, but the members can help you think through wills, bequests, life insurance, and other sorts of planned giving.

Mega Gifts: Who gives them, who gets them
Jerold Panas
Precept Press
169 East Illinois Street
Chicago, IL 60611

Pinpointing Affluence
Dr. Judith Nichols, CFRE
Precept Press
169 East Illinois Street
Chicago, IL 60611

How to use demographics and psychographics to identify and cultivate the 19 million Americans capable of giving gifts of $1,000 to $100,000.

Planned Giving for the One Person Development Office
Deferred Giving Services
614 West South Hale Street
Wheaton, IL 60187

An extremely useful tool by David Schmeling, CFRE. Information on marketing plans, recruiting key board members, preparing a budget, integrating and marketing planned giving, sample forms and letters.

The Seven Faces of Philanthropy: A New Approach to
Cultivating Major Donors
Russ Alan Prince and Karen Maru File
Jossey-Bass Publishers
350 Sansome Street
San Francisco, CA
Tel: (415) 433-1740
Fax: (415) 433-0499

Based on extensive research with extremely wealthy people, the authors describe seven personality profiles, and how to work with each type of donor.

240

Take the Fear Out of Asking for Major Gifts
James A. Donovan
Donovan Management Inc. (1993)
4744 Hall Road
Orlando, FL 32817
Tel: (800) 247-3023

A guide for professional staff and trustees of non-profit organizations with step-by-step instructions, self-study exercises, checklists, charts, and graphs. Quantity discounts available.

We Gave Away A Fortune
Christophr Mogil and Anne Slepian
New Society Publishers
4527 Springfield Avenue
Philadelphia PA 19143

or
P.O. Box 189
Gabriola Island BC V0R 1X0

Where the Money Is: A Fund Raiser's Guide to the Rich
Helen Bergan
BioGuide Press
(Second Edition, 1992)
P.O. Box 16072
Alexandria, VA 22302
Tel: (703) 820-9045

Emphasizes prospect and donor research in pursuit of donations from the rich.

k. MEDIA

Sources: The Directory of Contacts for Editors, Reporters and Researchers
9 St. Nicholas Street, Suite 402
Toronto, ON M4Y 1W5
(406) 964-7799

Sent free to journalists semi-annually. You pay to be listed. Vital if you want writers to contact you when they are working on news or feature stories.

l. STATISTICS

Canada's Charitable Economy: Its Role and Contribution
Larry W. Smith (Department of Economics,
University of Waterloo)
The Canadian Foundation for Economic Education
2 St. Clair Avenue West, #501
Toronto, ON M4V 1L5
Tel: (416) 968-2236
Fax: (416) 968-0488

Comprehensive analysis of donors, donations, volunteers, charitable organizations, etc.

m. VOLUNTEERS

Development and Direction for Boards of Directors
John E. Tropman
Canadian Centre for Philanthropy
1329 Bay Street, Suite 200
Toronto, ON M5R 2C4
Tel: (416) 515-0764
Fax: (416) 515-0773

Learn a revolutionary and effective method for running board meetings that result in high-quality decision-making. Exercises to evaluate your board and its operations.

Promoting Volunteerism
Janet Lautenschlager
Canadian Identity Directorate
Department of Canadian Heritage
Ottawa, ON K1A 0M5
Fax: (819) 953-4131

Strategies and approaches to promoting volunteerism. Includes list of reference tools on public relations, publicity, media relations, and public education and how to buy or borrow them.

The Successful Volunteer Organization
Joan Flanagan
Contemporary Books
180 North Stetson Avenue
Chicago, IL 60601
Tel: (800) 621-1918
Fax: (800) 998-3103

In Canada:
Fitzhenry & Whiteside
195 Allstate Parkway
Markham, ON L3R 4T8
(905) 477-9700

Currently out of print. It's worth looking for in your public or university library.

Working with Volunteer Boards
Volunteer Ontario
2 Dunbloor Road, Suite 203
Etobicoke, ON M9A 2E4
Tel: (416) 236-0588
Fax: (416) 236-0590

n. VIDEO

"Ask Somebody for Money Today." The best of Joan Flanagan's workshops. Three one-hour fundraising training videotapes: Getting Started; Asking for Money; and Fundraising forever.

The tapes are $30 each. The complete set of all three tapes, including training manuals, are $75. Available from:

Partners in Caregiving Program
Department of Psychiatry and Behavioral Medicine
The Bowman Gray School of Medicine
Medical Center Boulevard
Winston-Salem, NC 27157-1087
Tel: (910) 716-4941

"The Fund Raising Game" is a video education tool with 270-page handbook designed for volunteers, board, and staff in all kinds of charities and non-profit groups. It was produced by The Trillium Foundation of Ontario and TVOntario.

Host and creative consultant Ken Wyman offers his own expert advice, while tips and strategies from experienced fundraisers help reinforce important fundraising principles. The series is closed captioned. For details and order form, contact Ken Wyman & Associates in Toronto.

MOTIVATING AND MANAGING TODAY'S VOLUNTEERS

How to build and lead a terrific team

by Flora MacLeod

$11.95

People volunteer to contribute in a meaningful way to the community. Yet many new and long-time volunteers end up quitting; They feel their ideas and expertise are neither considered nor valued. Managing volunteers and making sure they feel they are full-fledged contributors to the organization is a full-time job. This book will help you hire a volunteer program manager and set up a program that organizes, evaluates, and recognizes your volunteers.

- Learn why organizations that haven't used volunteers before are now seeking them out
- Discover how a program manager can help keep volunteers organized and productive
- Take the steps to finding and hiring the ideal manager for your group's volunteer program
- Learn how to keep track of your current volunteers
- Attract the right volunteers to your organization

ORDER FORM

All prices are subject to change without notice. Books are available in book, department, and stationery stores. If you cannot buy the book through a store, please use this order form. (Please print.)

Name _____

Address _____

_____

Charge to: ❑ Visa ❑ MasterCard

Credit Card # _____

Expiration Date _____

Signature _____

YES, please send me:

_____ copies of **Motivating and Managing Today's Volunteers**, $11.95

_____ copies of **Forming and Managing a Non-Profit Organization in Canada**, $19.95 (Canada only)

Please add $3.00 for postage & handling. Canadian residents, please add 7% GST to your order. WA residents, please add 7.8% sales tax.

❑ **Check here for a free catalogue.**

IN CANADA
Please send your order to the nearest location:

Self-Counsel Press
1481 Charlotte Road
North Vancouver, B.C.
V7J 1H1

Self-Counsel Press
4 Bram Court
Brampton, Ontario
L6W 3R2

IN THE U.S.A.
Please send your order to:

Self-Counsel Press Inc.
1704 N. State Street
Bellingham, WA 98225